Walking Through The Word

A Church-Based Academic Bible Survey of the Old and New Testament

Written by Prophetess Tamiya Lewis

Copyright © 2025 Tamiya D. Lewis
All rights reserved.

ISBN: 978-1-7351403-0-8

Dedication

This work is dedicated to believers everywhere who desire to grow deeper in their understanding of God's Word.

Among the major world religions, Christianity often reflects a noticeable gap in the consistent and intentional study of its foundational texts. While many adherents of other faiths devote themselves to learning both their own doctrines and those of others, Christians are sometimes less disciplined in this vital pursuit.

It is my prayer that this book serves as a call to return to the Scriptures with renewed passion and purpose. May it inspire a generation of believers who are rooted in truth, strengthened in faith, and equipped for effective ministry through diligent study of the Bible—the living Word of God. To the glory of God and the edification of His Church.

Table of Contents

Dedication 4

Preface 9

Part I – The Pentateuch (Genesis–Deuteronomy) 30

Part II – The Historical Books (Joshua–Esther) 43

Part III – The Poetic and Wisdom Books (Job–Song of Solomon) 54

Part IV – The Major Prophets (Isaiah–Daniel) 67

Part V – The Minor Prophets (Hosea–Malachi) 78

Part VI – The Gospels (Matthew–John) 87

Part VII – The Acts of the Apostles 99

Part VIII – The Pauline Epistles (Romans–Philemon) 106

Part IX – The General Epistles (Hebrews–Jude) 111

Part IX – The Pastoral Epistles (Timothy–Titus) 114

Part X – The Revelation of Jesus Christ 120

Bonus Material.. 123

Preface

The Bible Survey: Walking Through The Word— the Old and New Testaments Complete Study Volume has been developed as a comprehensive academic and church-based study guide. This work seeks to provide students, ministers, and Christian educators with a structured exploration of Scripture from Genesis to Revelation. The intent of this survey is to bridge biblical history, theology, and spiritual formation within the context of the local church.

The study approach emphasizes both historical context and doctrinal significance, integrating faith and scholarship in a way that honors the authority of the Word of God. Each section presents the historical background, major themes, theological insights, and Christ-centered applications found in every book of the Bible.

Special acknowledgment is given to the Sanctuary Evangelistic Church, where this vision for biblical education and discipleship was cultivated, and to the faculty and community of Oral Roberts University, whose commitment to academic excellence and spiritual empowerment continues to inspire. May this work strengthen the body of Christ and contribute to a deeper understanding of God's revelation through His Word.

How To Study The Bible

Studying the Bible well means more than just reading it; it's about engaging with Scripture thoughtfully, prayerfully, and systematically so you can understand **what it says**, **what it means**, and **how it applies to life today**.

Here's a structured approach you can follow:

---

1. Pray First

Begin with prayer, asking the Holy Spirit for understanding (John 14:26).

Example: "Lord, open my eyes to see the truth in Your Word and help me apply it."

---

2. Choose a Method of Study

There are several ways to study the Bible, depending on your goal:

a. Book Study

Study one book at a time (e.g., Gospel of John, Romans, or Psalms).

- Read the whole book to get context.
- Identify the main theme and key verses.
- Take notes on what stands out.

b. Topical Study

Study what the Bible says about a specific topic (e.g., forgiveness, faith, love, Holy Spirit).

- Use a concordance or Bible app to find all verses on that topic.
- Compare passages to see how Scripture interprets itself.

c. Character Study

Examine the life of a biblical figure (e.g., Moses, Ruth, Paul).

- Note their strengths, weaknesses, challenges, and relationship with God.
- Ask what lessons you can learn from their life.
-

d. Verse-by-Verse or Inductive Study

Go slowly through a passage and analyze it carefully.
Use the **Inductive Bible Study Method**:

1. **Observation** – What does the text *say*? (Who, what, when, where, why, how?)
2. **Interpretation** – What does it *mean*? (What did it mean to the original audience?)
3. **Application** – How does it *apply* to my life today?

---

3. Use the Right Tools

Helpful resources include:

- **Study Bible** (NIV, ESV, or CSB Study Bible)
- **Concordance** (Strong's Exhaustive Concordance)
- **Bible Dictionary** (Nelson's Illustrated Bible Dictionary)
- **Commentaries** (Believers Bible Commentary)
- **Maps and timelines**
- **Bible software or apps** (e.g., Blue Letter Bible, Logos, YouVersion)
- **Bible Handbook** (Holman Illustrated Bible Handbook)

---

4. Consider the Context

Always read in context — what comes before and after a verse matters.
Ask:

- Who wrote this book?
- Who was the audience?
- Why was this book written?
- Key scripture every book
- Who are the major players?
- When was the book written?
- What are the major events of every chapter?
- What was going on in history that might have influenced this book?

---

5. Take Notes and Journal

Write down insights, key verses, and personal reflections.
Keeping a "Bible Study Journal" helps you track your spiritual growth and prayers.

6. Apply What You Learn

The goal of study isn't just knowledge — it's transformation (James 1:22).
Ask:

- How can I live this truth today?
- What does this teach me about God's character?

7. Study with Others

Join a Bible study group, church class, or online community.
Discussing Scripture with others deepens understanding and accountability.

PRE-TEST

Instructions
This pretest is designed to help us understand your current level of Bible knowledge before we begin our study. It is **not** graded and will not affect your participation in any way. Your responses simply help us tailor the teaching to best serve you. Answers can be found on page `139.

1. Name two Patriarchs?

2. How many books are in the Old Testament?
3. Psalms is divided into how many sections?
4. Who wrote the largest number of books in the Old Testament?
5. Who was the first prophet in the Old Testament?
6. Name one of God's covenantal names?
7. Who was the 1st King of Israel?
8. Write one scripture in the book of psalms?

9. What is the longest book in the Old Testament?
10. Who was the richest King in the Old Testament?
11. Who is known as "a man after God's own heart?"
12. What is the difference between the major and the minor prophets?

13. Which book of the bible focuses on the Holy Spirit?
14. What is the purpose of the gospels?

15. How many books are in the New Testament?
16. What is an Epistle?

17. Name two epistles?

18. How many gospels are there?
19. Who wrote the largest number of books in the New Testament?
20. What is an apostle?

21. Name 4 key figures in the New Testament?

Background of the Old Testament

I. Purpose and Reason It Was Written

Key Idea:

The Old Testament was written to reveal **who God is**, **how He relates to His people**, and **His plan of redemption** for all humanity.

Before God called Abraham, the nations of the world lived in spiritual darkness—worshiping many false gods and idols. Through Abraham, God began forming a covenant people who would come to know Him as the one true and living God.

II. Key Scripture Passages

1. The Call of Abram — Genesis 12:1–3

"The Lord had said to Abram, 'Leave your native country, your relatives, and your father's family, and go to the land that I will show you.
I will make you into a great nation. I will bless you and make you famous, and you will be a blessing to others.
I will bless those who bless you and curse those who treat you with contempt. All the families on earth will be blessed through you.'"

Summary:

- God called Abram to leave his homeland and trust in His promise.
- God established a covenant to make Abram the father of a great nation.
- Through Abram's descendants, **all nations of the earth** would be blessed.
- This blessing ultimately pointed to **Jesus Christ**, the promised Savior.

---

2. The Covenant with Abraham — Genesis 17:4–6

"This is my covenant with you: I will make you the father of a multitude of nations!
What's more, I am changing your name. It will no longer be Abram. Instead, you will be called Abraham, for you will be the father of many nations.
I will make you extremely fruitful. Your descendants will become many nations, and kings will be among them!"

Summary:

- God reaffirmed His covenant by changing Abram's name to **Abraham** ("father of many").
- The covenant promised fruitfulness, nations, and royal lineage.
- God's plan expanded beyond Israel—His desire was to reach **all nations** through Abraham's faith.

III. Theological Themes

Theme	Explanation	Scripture Reference
Covenant Relationship	God established a binding relationship with His people, built on promise and faithfulness.	Genesis 17:4–6
Monotheism	The Old Testament reveals the one true God amidst a world of idolatry.	Deuteronomy 6:4
Faith and Obedience	Abraham's faith became the model for all believers.	Genesis 15:6; Romans 4:3
Blessing to the Nations	God's redemptive plan was global from the start, fulfilled through Christ.	Genesis 12:3; Galatians 3:8–9

IV. Key Takeaways

- The Old Testament records God's **progressive revelation**—how He made Himself known to humanity over time.
- It establishes the **foundation of God's covenant**, preparing the way for the New Testament.
- Abraham's faith and obedience demonstrate that relationship with God is built on **trust and surrender**, not ritual alone.
- The promise to Abraham finds its ultimate fulfillment in **Jesus Christ**, who brings salvation to all nations.

Breakdown of the Old Testament

Genesis Exodus Leviticus Numbers Deuteronomy	**LAW**
Joshua Judges Ruth I Samuel II Samuel I Kings II Kings I Chronicles II Chronicles Ezra Nehemiah Esther	**HISTORY**
Job Psalms Proverbs Ecclesiastes Song of Solomon	**POETRY AND WISDOM**
Isaiah Jeremiah Lamentations Ezekiel Daniel	**MAJOR PROPHETS**
Hosea Joel Amos Obadiah Jonah Micah Nahum Habakkuk Zephaniah Haggai Zechariah Malachi	**MINOR PROPHETS**

God: The Gangster of the Old Testament

Formal Introduction

Nile turned to Blood	Exodus 7:14-25	Khnum: guardian of the Nile Hapi: spirit of the Nile Osiris: Nile was bloodstream
Frogs	Exodus 8:1-15	Heqt: form of frog; god of resurrection
Gnats	Exodus 8:16-19	
Flies	Exodus 8:20-32	
Plague on Cattle	Exodus 9:1-7	Hathor: mother-godess; form of cow Apis: bull of God Ptah; symbol of fertility Mnevis: sacred bull of Helopolis
Boils	Exodus 9:8-12	Imhotep: god of medicine
Hail	Exodus 9:13-35	Nut: sky goddess Isis: godess of life Seth: protector of crops
Locusts	Exodus 10:1-20	Isis: goddess f life Seth: protector of crops
Darkness	Exodus 10:21-29	Re, Aten, Atum, Horus: all sun gods of sorts
Death of First Born	Exodus 11:1-12:36	The deity of Pharaoh: Osiris, the giver of life

False Gods and the Power of the True God

I. Dagon: The God of Grain

Key Passage: 1 Samuel 5:4–7

Dagon had fallen face down before the Ark of the Lord again. This time his head and hands had broken off and were lying in the doorway... The Lord's heavy hand struck the people of Ashdod and the nearby villages with a plague of tumors. The people cried out, "We can't keep the Ark of the God of Israel here any longer! He is against us! We will all be destroyed along with Dagon, our god."

Background:

- **Dagon** was worshiped as the Philistine **god of grain and fertility**.
- The **Philistines**, known for agriculture, prayed to Dagon for abundant harvests.
- When the **Ark of the Covenant** (representing God's presence) was captured and placed in Dagon's temple, the idol was destroyed.

God's Message:

- **Dagon's head** broken → God removed false **authority and leadership**.
- **Dagon's hands** broken → God removed false **power and ability to provide**.
- God revealed that **He alone controls prosperity, strength, and life**.

II. Baal: The God of Storms

Key Passage: 1 Kings 18:20–24, 33–39

Elijah said, "How long will you waver between two opinions? If the Lord is God, follow Him! But if Baal is God, follow him!"
The prophets of Baal called on their god all day with no answer.
Elijah prayed once, and the fire of the Lord fell from heaven, consuming the sacrifice, the wood, the stones, and the water.
The people fell on their faces and cried, "The Lord—He is God!"

Background:

- **Baal** was believed to control **rain, storms, and lightning**.
- King Ahab and Queen Jezebel led Israel into **Baal worship**, turning the nation away from God.
- On **Mount Carmel**, Elijah challenged 450 prophets of Baal to prove who the real God was.

God's Message:

- God answered **by fire**, defeating Baal on his own turf (lightning).
- The miracle showed that **the Creator controls creation**, not idols.
- Through Elijah's obedience, the people's hearts were turned back to the Lord.

III. Timeline: God's Superiority Over False Gods

Event	Approx. Date	False God / System	Location	God's Demonstration of Power	Key Lesson
The Plagues of Egypt	c. 1450 BC	Egyptian gods (Ra, Hapi, etc.)	Egypt	Ten plagues directly challenged Egypt's deities.	God rules over all creation and nations.
The Fall of Dagon	c. 1050 BC	Dagon – god of grain	Ashdod (Philistia)	Idol fell and broke before the Ark of the Lord.	No idol can stand before the presence of God.
Mount Carmel Showdown	c. 850 BC	Baal – god of storms	Mount Carmel (Israel)	Fire from heaven consumed the sacrifice.	God alone is worthy of worship.
The Exile and Return	586–516 BC	Babylonian and Persian gods	Babylon & Judah	God preserved His people despite foreign powers.	God's sovereignty extends beyond borders.
The Coming of Christ	1st Century AD	Roman gods and emperor worship	Roman Empire	Christ's resurrection defeated sin, death, and idolatry.	The ultimate victory belongs to God alone.

IV. Comparison Table: Dagon vs. Baal

Aspect	Dagon	Baal
Type of God	God of grain, agriculture	God of storms, rain, and fertility
Worshipers	Philistines	Canaanites and Israelites under Ahab
God's Response	Idol fell; head and hands broken	Fire consumed the altar at Elijah's prayer
Symbolic Message	God removed false provision and power	God revealed true control over nature and power
Spiritual Outcome	Philistines feared the God of Israel	Israelites repented and declared, "The Lord—He is God!"

V. Key Takeaways

- God's power exposes the weakness of idols—ancient and modern.
- Every false god promises control, prosperity, or pleasure—but only the Lord provides true life and authority.
- The presence of God cannot coexist with idolatry; it always demands **repentance and reverence**.
- Elijah's boldness and God's victory remind believers to **stand firm in faith** even when outnumbered or opposed.

Theophanies in Genesis

I AM YHWH	I AM EL SHADDAI
Initiation of agreement	Initiation of fulfillment
Abraham	
Genesis 15:7 Occasion: ratification of covenant Emphasis Giving of land	Genesis 17: 1-8 Occasion Indication of acceptance of covenant (circumcision) Acts name change; Isaac promised with year Emphasis Many descendants, nations, kings will come from you
Jacob	
Genesis 28:13-15 Occasion First promise of covenant blessings To Jacob Emphasis: Bringing him back to land and giving it to him	Genesis 35: 10-12 Occasion: Indication of acceptance of covenant (destruction of foreign gods, pillar set up) Accepts name change Emphasis: Many descendants, nations, kings will come from you

A **theophany** is a visible manifestation of God, often taking a tangible or perceivable form such as a burning bush, a storm, a cloud, a pillar of fire, or appearing in human or angelic form. These manifestations serve to reveal God's presence, communicate His will, and demonstrate His power and holiness to His people. Some theologians also consider certain appearances of the **"Angel of the Lord"** as theophanies, as this figure is sometimes understood to represent the pre-incarnate Christ.

Examples of Theophanies

- **The Burning Bush:** God appears to Moses in a bush that burns without being consumed, revealing His will and commissioning Moses to lead the Israelites out of Egypt.
- **The Pillar of Cloud and Fire:** In the wilderness, God guides the Israelites by appearing as a pillar of cloud by day and a pillar of fire by night.
- **The Angel of the Lord:** This recurring figure is sometimes identified as God Himself, as when He wrestles with Jacob, prompting Jacob to declare, "I have seen God face to face."
- **A Thunderstorm:** God appears to Job through a whirlwind or tempest, demonstrating His power and wisdom.
- **Appearance in Human Form:** God visits Abraham and Sarah as three visitors. The text emphasizes, "The Lord appeared to Abraham" (Genesis 18:1), and later addresses Abraham directly as the Lord.

Significance of Theophanies

- **Revelation of God's Presence:** Theophanies reveal God's active, immanent presence among humanity and His chosen people.
- **Communication of Divine Will:** They allow God to communicate directly with individuals or communities, often delivering instructions, guidance, or covenants.
- **Revelation of God's Holiness:** Theophanies highlight God's power and holiness, inspiring reverence and awe in those who encounter Him.
- **Foreshadowing Christ:** Many theologians see Old Testament theophanies—particularly those involving the Angel of the Lord—as prefiguring the ultimate theophany: the incarnation of Jesus Christ.

Types of Offerings

Name	Burnt portion	Other portion	Animals	Occasion or reason	Scriptural reference
Burnt Offering	All	None	Male without blemish, animal according to wealth	Propitiation for sin, demonstrates dedication	Leviticus 1
Meal offering	Token portion	Eaten by priest	Unleavened cakes or grains must be salted	General thankfulness for first fruits	Leviticus 2
Peace offering Thank offering Vow offering Freewill offering	Fat portions	Shared in fellowship meal by priest and offerer	Male or female without blemish according to wealth; freewill: slight blemish allowed	Fellowship For an unexpected blessing For deliverance when a vow was made on that condition For general thankfulness	Leviticus 3 Leviticus 22:18-30
Sin Offering	Fat portion	Eaten by priest	Priest or congregation bull king; he goat individual she goat	Applies basically to situation where purification is needed	Leviticus 4
Guilt offering	Fat portion	Eaten by priest	Ram without blemish	An object of guilt or desecration or desacralization of something holy	Leviticus 5:6,7

Clean and Unclean Animals

Classes	Clean	Unclean

Mammals	Two qualifications
	  1. Cloven hoofs
	  2. Chewing of the cud
	Leviticus 11:3-7 and Duet. 14:6-8
		Carnivores and those not meeting both clean qualification

Birds	Those not specifically listed as forbidden	Birds of prey or scavengers Lev. 11:13-19 Deut. 14:11-20
Reptiles	None	All Leviticus 11:29, 30

Water Animals	Two qualifications:
	  1. Fins
	  2. Scales
	  3. Leviticus 11:9-12 Duet 14:9,10
		Those not meeting both "clean qualifications

Insects	Those in the grasshopper family Leviticus 11:20-23	Winged quadrupeds

Why Was Moses Chosen to Write Several Books in the Old Testament

Moses was chosen to write most of the Old Testament—specifically the first five books, known as the **Torah** (Hebrew) or **Pentateuch** (Greek) these books consist of Genesis, Exodus, Leviticus, Numbers, and Deuteronomy—because of his **unique relationship with God**, his **leadership role**, and his **divine calling** as both **prophet and lawgiver**.

1. Divine Appointment
- **God personally chose Moses** to lead Israel out of Egypt and to deliver His laws to the people.
- In **Exodus 24:4**, it says, *"Moses wrote all the words of the Lord."*
- He didn't write by his own authority, but under **divine inspiration** — guided by the Holy Spirit to record God's revelation faithfully.

2. Direct Communication with God
- Unlike other prophets who received visions or dreams, Moses **spoke with God "face to face"** (Exodus 33:11; Numbers 12:6–8).
- This unique level of intimacy made him the ideal person to receive and record God's instructions, laws, and historical dealings with Israel.

3. Eyewitness of Major Events
- Moses was a **firsthand witness** to the events of the Exodus, the giving of the Law at Mount Sinai, and Israel's wilderness journey.
- As both participant and leader, he could **accurately record** God's acts, Israel's covenant history, and the moral lessons they revealed.

4. Lawgiver and Covenant Mediator
- Moses served as the **mediator of the Old Covenant** between God and Israel.
- The Pentateuch lays out the foundation of that covenant — laws, worship instructions, and moral principles — all given through Moses.

5. Educational and Leadership Role
- Raised in Pharaoh's palace (Exodus 2:10), Moses was **educated in Egyptian wisdom** and skilled in writing and administration (Acts 7:22).
- This background equipped him to **organize, record, and teach** Israel's spiritual and legal framework.

6. Preserving God's Story and Covenant
- Through Moses' writings, God established a **permanent record** of His creation, promises, and covenant relationship with humanity.
- His writings set the **theological and moral foundation** for the rest of Scripture and for the coming of Christ.

Summary Chart

Reason	Description	Key Scriptures
Divine Appointment	God chose Moses to record His Word	Exodus 24:4; Deuteronomy 31:9
Direct Revelation	Spoke with God "face to face"	Numbers 12:6–8; Exodus 33:11
Eyewitness of Events	Lived through the Exodus and wilderness period	Exodus–Deuteronomy
Lawgiver & Mediator	Delivered and recorded God's covenant law	Exodus 19–24
Educated Leader	Trained in writing and leadership	Acts 7:22
Covenant Record Keeper	Preserved God's history and promises	Deuteronomy 31:24–26

The Covenantal Names of God

I. Introduction

When God introduced Himself to the Israelites, He showed them one of His characteristics and then taught them how to develop a relationship with Him based off the name given to that characteristic. This taught the Israel how to develop a relationship with him, by causing them to identify His power, applying the covenant and compare it to their need. (Lewis, 2017)

A. Purpose of the Study
- To understand God's character through His covenantal names
- To see how each name reveals a unique aspect of God's relationship with His people
- To help believers grow in confidence, worship, and spiritual identity

B. Importance of God's Names in Scripture
- In biblical times, names revealed nature, purpose, and authority
- God reveals His names in moments of covenant interaction
- Each name reveals how He cares for His people

II. Overview of the Covenant Name: YHWH (Yahweh)

A. Meaning of Yahweh
- "I AM WHO I AM" (Exodus 3:14)
- Self-existing, eternal, unchanging

B. Yahweh as a Covenant Name
- The name God uses when promising, delivering, and redeeming His people
- Every compound name flows from Yahweh

III. The Covenantal Names of God Jehovah or Yahweh is traditionally used first.

1. Yahweh-Jireh — "The Lord Will Provide"
Text: Genesis 22:14
Context: Abraham's test with Isaac
Covenantal Focus: God meets needs before we see the solution
Teaching Emphasis:
- God provides materially, spiritually, and sacrificially
- Foreshadows Christ as God's ultimate provision

2. Yahweh-Rapha — "The Lord Who Heals"
Text: Exodus 15:26
Context: God heals bitter waters at Marah
Covenantal Focus: Healing comes through obedience and relationship
Teaching Emphasis:
- God heals body, mind, soul, and community
- Healing is part of God's covenant care

3. Yahweh-Nissi — "The Lord Is My Banner"
Text: Exodus 17:15
Context: Victory over Amalek
Covenantal Focus: God is our victory and covering
Teaching Emphasis:
- God fights for His people
- Our strength and protection come from Him

4. Yahweh-M'Kaddish — "The Lord Who Sanctifies You"
Text: Exodus 31:13; Leviticus 20:8
Context: Instructions on holiness
Covenantal Focus: God sets His people apart
Teaching Emphasis:
- Sanctification is God's work in us
- Holiness is relational, not just behavioral

5. Yahweh-Shalom — "The Lord Is Peace"
Text: Judges 6:24
Context: Gideon's fear and calling
Covenantal Focus: Peace in moments of fear and calling
Teaching Emphasis:
- God's peace is wholeness, not the absence of problems
- Peace comes through His presence

6. Yahweh-Sabaoth — "The Lord of Hosts"
Text: 1 Samuel 1:3; Psalm 24:10
Context: God as commander of angelic armies
Covenantal Focus: Divine protection and authority
Teaching Emphasis:
- God rules over earthly and heavenly kingdoms
- Nothing is beyond His power

7. Yahweh-Ra'ah — "The Lord Is My Shepherd"
Text: Psalm 23:1
Context: David's experience with God
Covenantal Focus: God guides, protects, and provides
Teaching Emphasis:
- God leads His people personally
- He knows His sheep by name

8. Yahweh-Tsidkenu — "The Lord Our Righteousness"
Text: Jeremiah 23:6; 33:16
Context: Prophetic word about the coming Messiah
Covenantal Focus: Righteousness provided through Christ
Teaching Emphasis:
- We cannot establish righteousness on our own
- Christ fulfills the covenant as our righteousness

9. Yahweh-Shammah — "The Lord Is There"
Text: Ezekiel 48:35
Context: Vision of the restored city
Covenantal Focus: God's abiding presence
Teaching Emphasis:
- God is permanently present with His people
- Fulfilled in the Holy Spirit and future Kingdom

Part I
The Old Testament

Pentateuch or Torah

Genesis

Classification: Law / Torah

Author: Traditionally Moses

Date of Composition: ca. 1450–1400 B.C. (during Israel's wilderness period)

Historical Context: Covers creation to the migration of Jacob's family to Egypt (ca. 4000–1800 B.C.)

Purpose and Theme

Genesis introduces the origin of the universe, humanity, sin, nations, and Israel. It records God's covenant with Abraham and establishes the foundation for His redemptive plan to separate a people unto himself.

Theme: Beginnings — God's sovereign creation and covenant promises.

Structure

1. Primeval History (Chs. 1–11): Creation, Fall, Flood, Babel.
2. Patriarchal History (Chs. 12–50): Abraham, Isaac, Jacob, Joseph.

Key Scriptures

- Genesis 1:1 – "In the beginning God created the heavens and the earth."
- Genesis 3:15 – Protoevangelium (first gospel promise).
- Genesis 12:1–3 – The Abrahamic Covenant.
- Genesis 50:20 – God's providence in human events.

Key Words / Concepts

- "Beginnings" (Hebrew: bereshith)
- Covenant (berith)

- Blessing
- Promise

Major Figures

Adam, Noah, Abraham, Sarah, Isaac, Jacob (Israel), Joseph.

Timeline / Setting

Creation → Flood → Tower of Babel → Patriarchs (Abraham to Joseph) → Israelites in Egypt.

OUTLINE
- Creation 1:1-2:25
- Fall of humanity 3:1-6:8
- Flood
- Patriarchs (Abraham, Isaac, Jacob)
- Joseph in Egypt

Exodus

Classification: Law / Torah

Author: Moses

Date of Composition: ca. 1450–1400 B.C.

Historical Context: Israel's deliverance from Egypt (ca. 1446 B.C.) and covenant formation at Sinai.

Purpose and Theme

Reveals God as Deliverer and Covenant Maker.

The Exodus event is central to Israel's identity and theology—God redeems His people by blood and power.

Theme: Redemption and Covenant Relationship.

Structure

1. Deliverance from Egypt (1–18)
2. Covenant at Sinai (19–24)
3. Instructions for Worship / Tabernacle (25–40)

Key Scriptures

- Exodus 3:14 – "I AM WHO I AM."
- Exodus 12:13 – The blood of the Passover lamb.
- Exodus 19:5–6 – Israel as a kingdom of priests.
- Exodus 20 – The Ten Commandments.

Key Words / Concepts

- Redemption
- Deliverance

- Covenant
- Law (Torah)
- Presence (Tabernacle symbol).

Major Figures

Moses, Aaron, Pharaoh, Miriam, Joshua.

Timeline / Setting

Slavery in Egypt → Plagues and Passover → Exodus (c. 1446 B.C.) → Mount Sinai → Tabernacle built.

Leviticus

Classification: Law / Torah

Author: Moses

Date of Composition: ca. 1445 B.C. (shortly after Exodus)

Historical Context: Israel encamped at Mount Sinai, learning how to live as God's holy nation.

Purpose and Theme

Leviticus is a manual for holiness, worship, and priestly service.

It outlines sacrificial systems, purity laws, and moral codes emphasizing God's holiness and Israel's separation.

Theme: Holiness in Worship and Daily Life.

Structure

1. Laws of Sacrifice and Worship (1–10)
2. Laws of Purity and Atonement (11–16)
3. Holiness Code (17–27)

Key Scriptures

- Leviticus 11:44 – "Be holy, for I am holy."
- Leviticus 16 – Day of Atonement (Yom Kippur).
- Leviticus 17:11 – "The life of the flesh is in the blood."

Key Words / Concepts

- Holiness (qodesh)
- Atonement (kippur)
- Sacrifice (korban)
- Priesthood

Major Figures

Moses, Aaron, Nadab, Abihu.

Timeline / Setting

Covers roughly one month between Exodus and Numbers while Israel remains at Sinai.

Numbers

Classification: Law / Torah

Author: Moses

Date of Composition: ca. 1406 B.C.

Historical Context: The 40-year wilderness journey from Sinai to Moab.

Purpose and Theme

Records the testing, rebellion, and perseverance of Israel in the wilderness. Demonstrates God's faithfulness in discipline and guidance.

Theme: From Sinai to the Promised Land — Faith in God's Promise.

Structure

1. Preparation and Census at Sinai (1–10)
2. Rebellion and Wandering (11–25)
3. New Generation and Renewal of Hope (26–36)

Key Scriptures

- Numbers 6:24–26 – The Priestly Blessing.
- Numbers 14:22–23 – Judgment on unbelief.
- Numbers 21:8–9 – The bronze serpent (a type of Christ).

Key Words / Concepts

- Wilderness
- Testing

- Faithfulness
- Promise

Major Figures

Moses, Aaron, Miriam, Joshua, Caleb, Balaam.

Timeline / Setting

Covers approximately 38 years (1446–1406 B.C.) of Israel's wandering.

Deuteronomy

Classification: Law / Torah

Author: Moses (completed by Joshua after Moses' death)

Date of Composition: ca. 1406 B.C.

Historical Context: Final address to the second generation before entering Canaan.

Purpose and Theme

Deuteronomy is a covenant renewal document, reaffirming the Law for a new generation. It emphasizes obedience, love for God, and remembrance of His works.

Theme: Covenant Renewal and Preparation for Promise.

Structure

1. Historical Prologue and Review (1–4)
2. Covenant Laws and Exhortations (5–26)
3. Blessings and Curses (27–30)
4. Farewell and Death of Moses (31–34)

Key Scriptures

- Deuteronomy 6:4–5 – The Shema ("Hear, O Israel…").
- Deuteronomy 8:3 – "Man shall not live by bread alone."
- Deuteronomy 30:19–20 – Choose life and obedience.

Key Words / Concepts

- Covenant
- Obedience
- Remembrance
- Love (ḥesed)

Major Figures

Moses, Joshua

Timeline / Setting

Covers approximately one month on the plains of Moab (1406 B.C.), immediately before the conquest of Canaan.

Summary of the Pentateuch/Torah

Book	Theme	Date (B.C.)	Setting	Key Figures	Key Scripture
Genesis	Beginnings: Creation and Covenant	c. 4000-1800	Mesopotamia to Egypt	Adam, Abraham, Joseph	Gen 12:1-3
Exodus	Redemption and Law	c. 1446	Egypt and Sinai	Moses, Pharaoh	Ex 19:5,6
Leviticus	Holiness and Worship	c. 1445	Sinai	Aaron, Priests	Lev 19:2
Numbers	Testing and Faithfulness	1446-1406	Wilderness	Moses, Joshua	Num 6:24-26
Deuteronomy	Covenant Renewal	c. 1406	Moab	Moses, Joshua	Deut 6:4,5

Historical Books

Joshua

Classification: Historical
Author: Traditionally Joshua (with later editorial additions)
Date of Composition: ca. 1400–1370 B.C.
Historical Context: Israel enters and conquers the Promised Land after Moses' death.

Purpose and Theme

Joshua records the **fulfillment of God's promises to the patriarchs** through the conquest and settlement of Canaan.
Theme: *God's faithfulness in giving the land to His covenant people.*

Structure

1. **Conquest of Canaan** (1–12)

2. **Division of the Land** (13–22)

3. **Covenant Renewal** (23–24)

Key Scriptures

- Joshua 1:9 – "Be strong and courageous; do not be afraid."

- Joshua 24:15 – "Choose this day whom you will serve."

Key Words / Concepts
- *Covenant fulfillment*
- *Faithfulness*
- *Leadership transition*

Major Figures

Joshua, Caleb, Rahab, Achan.

Timeline / Setting

Conquest and settlement of Canaan (ca. 1406–1375 B.C.).

Judges

Classification: Historical
Author: Traditionally Samuel
Date of Composition: ca. 1050–1000 B.C.
Historical Context: Period between Joshua and the monarchy; tribal confederacy with cyclical rebellion and deliverance.

Purpose and Theme

Judges depicts Israel's **cycle of sin, oppression, repentance, and deliverance** to highlight the consequences of covenant unfaithfulness.
Theme: *God raises deliverers to redeem His people despite their unfaithfulness.*

Structure

• Introduction to the cycles (1–3:6)

• Stories of major judges: Othniel, Ehud, Deborah, Gideon, Jephthah, Samson (3:7–16:31)

• Conclusion and moral collapse (17–21)

Key Scriptures

• Judges 2:16 – "The LORD raised up judges… to deliver them."

• Judges 21:25 – "In those days there was no king in Israel; everyone did what was right in his own eyes."

Key Words / Concepts
• *Covenant violation*
• *Deliverance*
• *Sin cycle*

Major Figures

Othniel, Ehud, Deborah, Gideon, Samson, Samuel (as transitional figure).

Timeline / Setting

Approx. 1375–1050 B.C., tribal confederacy period.

Ruth

Classification: Historical / Poetic
Author: Traditionally Samuel or an unknown chronicler
Date of Composition: ca. 1100–1000 B.C.
Historical Context: Set during the Judges' period; post-famine in Bethlehem.

Purpose and Theme

Ruth highlights **loyalty, providence, and the inclusion of a Gentile into God's covenant people.**
Theme: *God's providential care and the ancestry of David.*

Key Scriptures

- Ruth 1:16 – "Where you go I will go; your people shall be my people."

- Ruth 4:13–17 – Boaz redeems Ruth; birth of Obed, David's grandfather.

Key Words / Concepts

- *Redemption*

- *Faithfulness*

- *Providence*

Major Figures

Ruth, Naomi, Boaz, Obed.

Timeline / Setting

During the Judges (~1100 B.C.), Bethlehem in Judah.

1 & 2 Samuel

Classification: Historical
Author: Traditionally Samuel, with contributions by Nathan and Gad
Date of Composition: ca. 1050–1000 B.C.
Historical Context: Transition from tribal confederacy to monarchy in Israel.

Purpose and Theme

These books **trace the rise of the monarchy**, God's choice of king, and the consequences of obedience or rebellion.
Theme: *God's sovereignty and covenant faithfulness through leadership.*

Structure

- 1 Samuel: Samuel's ministry, Saul's reign (Chs. 1–31)
- 2 Samuel: David's reign (Chs. 1–24)

Key Scriptures

- 1 Samuel 16:7 – "Man looks at the outward appearance, but the LORD looks at the heart."
- 2 Samuel 7:12–16 – God's covenant with David.

Key Words / Concepts

- *Kingship*
- *Covenant*
- *Obedience vs. rebellion*

Major Figures

Samuel, Saul, David, Jonathan, Nathan.

Timeline / Setting

c. 1100–970 B.C., transition from tribal confederacy to united monarchy.

1 & 2 Kings

Classification: Historical
Author: Traditionally Jeremiah or unknown chronicler
Date of Composition: ca. 560–538 B.C.
Historical Context: United monarchy (David/Solomon) → Divided kingdoms → Exile of Israel and Judah.

Purpose and Theme

Document Israel and Judah's **rise, division, decline, and exile** as consequences of covenant unfaithfulness.
Theme: *Faithfulness to God determines national destiny.*

Key Scriptures

- 1 Kings 3:12 – God's gift of wisdom to Solomon.

- 2 Kings 17:13–23 – Israel's exile due to idolatry.

Key Words / Concepts

- *Monarchy*

- *Prophecy and judgment*

- *Idolatry*

Major Figures

Solomon, Rehoboam, Elijah, Elisha, Hezekiah, Josiah.

Timeline / Setting

c. 970–586 B.C., United and Divided Kingdoms; Northern Kingdom (Israel) and Southern Kingdom (Judah).

1 & 2 Chronicles

Classification: Historical
Author: Traditionally Ezra
Date of Composition: ca. 450–400 B.C.
Historical Context: Post-exilic Judah; emphasis on temple, priesthood, and Davidic lineage.

Purpose and Theme

Chronicles **reframes Israel's history from Adam to exile**, emphasizing **worship, temple, and covenant continuity**.
Theme: *God's faithfulness through proper worship and Davidic covenant.*

Key Scriptures

- 1 Chronicles 28:9 – "Serve Him with a whole heart."

- 2 Chronicles 7:14 – God's promise to forgive a repentant nation.

Key Words / Concepts

- *Worship*

- *Temple*

- *Covenant*

Major Figures

David, Solomon, Ezra, Hezekiah, Josiah.

Timeline / Setting

Creation to post-exilic Judah (~4000–400 B.C., focusing on Davidic era).

Ezra

Classification: Historical
Author: Ezra
Date of Composition: ca. 450–400 B.C.
Historical Context: Post-exilic period; return from Babylonian captivity.

Purpose and Theme

Ezra focuses on **restoration of Israel's covenant life**, including temple rebuilding and reform.
Theme: *Covenant restoration through law and worship.*

Key Scriptures

- Ezra 7:10 – "He set his heart to study the Law of the LORD and to do it."

- Ezra 9:10–15 – Confession and intercession for the people.

Key Words / Concepts

- *Restoration*

- *Law*

- *Repentance*

Major Figures

Ezra, Zerubbabel, Jeshua (Joshua the high priest).

Timeline / Setting

Return from Babylonian exile (~538–458 B.C.).

Nehemiah

Classification: Historical
Author: Nehemiah
Date of Composition: ca. 430–400 B.C.
Historical Context: Rebuilding Jerusalem's walls after the exile; spiritual and social reform.

Purpose and Theme

Nehemiah records **physical and spiritual restoration**, emphasizing God's sovereignty and covenant fidelity.
Theme: *Rebuilding and reform for covenant obedience.*

Key Scriptures

- Nehemiah 2:17–18 – "Let us rebuild… and their hands will be strengthened."

- Nehemiah 8:10 – "The joy of the LORD is your strength."

Key Words / Concepts

- *Restoration*

- *Reform*

- *Obedience*

Major Figures

Nehemiah, Ezra, Artaxerxes (Persian king).

Timeline / Setting

Rebuilding of Jerusalem (ca. 445–432 B.C.).

Esther

Classification: Historical / Narrative
Author: Unknown (traditionally Mordecai)
Date of Composition: ca. 480–460 B.C.
Historical Context: Persian Empire; Jews living in exile under King Ahasuerus (Xerxes I).

Purpose and Theme

Esther demonstrates **God's providence and preservation of His people** in a foreign land.
Theme: *Divine providence and deliverance through courage and faith.*

Key Scriptures

- Esther 4:14 – "For such a time as this."
- Esther 9:22 – Institution of the Feast of Purim.

Key Words / Concepts

- *Providence*
- *Courage*
- *Deliverance*

Major Figures

Esther, Mordecai, King Ahasuerus (Xerxes I), Haman.

Timeline / Setting

Persian Empire (c. 480–470 B.C.); Jews in Susa (Shushan).

Summary of the Historical Books (Joshua–Esther)

Book	Theme	Date (B.C.)	Setting	Key Figures	Key Scripture
Joshua	Conquest and Covenant Fulfillment	1400	Canaan	Joshua, Caleb	Joshua 1:9
Judges	Cycle of Sin and Deliverance	1375-1050	Canaan	Deborah, Gideon, Samson	Judges 2:16
Ruth	Loyalty and Providence	1100	Bethlehem	Ruth, Boaz	Ruth 1:16
1&2 Samuel	Rise of Monarchy	1100-970	Israel	Samuel, Saul, David	2 Sam 7:12-16
1&2 Kings	Divided Kingdom & Exile	970-586	Israel & Judah	Solomon, Elijah	2 Kings 17:13-23
1&2 Chronicles	Temple & Worship	450-400	Judah	David, Solomon	2 Chron 7:14
Ezra	Post-Exilic Restoration	450	Jerusalem	Ezra, Zerubbabel	Ezra 7:10
Nehemiah	Rebuilding & Reform	445-432	Jerusalem	Nehemiah, Ezra	Neh 2:17–18
Esther	Providence & Deliverance				

Poetic and Wisdom Books

Job

Classification: Wisdom / Poetic

Author: Unknown (traditionally Moses or an anonymous sage)

Date of Composition: ca. 2000–1000 B.C. (likely during or after the Patriarchal period)

Historical Context: Reflects a pre-Mosaic, patriarchal setting with a focus on suffering, divine justice, and human faith.

Purpose and Theme

Job explores the problem of suffering, divine justice, and human righteousness. It challenges simplistic interpretations of prosperity and punishment, emphasizing trust in God's sovereignty.

Theme: Faith and integrity amid unexplained suffering.

Structure

1. Prologue: Job's righteousness and calamity (1–2)
2. Dialogues: Job and friends on suffering (3–31)
3. Monologues: Elihu and God's response (32–42:6)
4. Epilogue: Restoration of Job's fortunes (42:7–17)

Key Scriptures

- Job 1:21 – "The LORD gave, and the LORD has taken away."
- Job 19:25 – "I know that my Redeemer lives."
- Job 42:2 – God's sovereignty affirmed.

Key Words / Concepts

- Suffering
- Righteousness
- Providence

- Divine sovereignty

Major Figures

Job, Eliphaz, Bildad, Zophar, Elihu, God.

Timeline / Setting

Patriarchal Era, likely in the land of Uz (~2000 B.C.).

Breakdown of Psalms

Introduction Psalms 1-2	Psalms 1 Ultimate vindication of the righteous Psalms 2. God's choice and defense of Israelite king	
Book	**Theme**	**Content**
Book 1 (1-41)	David's conflict with Saul	Many individuals laments; most psalms mention enemies
Book 2 (42-72)	David's Kingship	Key psalms: 45, 48, 51, 54-64 mostly laments and enemy psalms
Book 3 (73-89)	Eighth century Assyrian crisis	Asaph and sons of Korah collections; key psalms 78
Book 4 (90-106)	Introspection about the destruction of the temple and exile	Praise collection 95-100; key psalms 90, 103-105
Book 5 (107-145)	Praise/reflection on return from exile and beginning of a new era	Hallelujah collection: 111-117 Songs of Ascent: 120-134 Davidic reprise 138-145 key psalms 107, 110, 119
Conclusion Book 5 (146-150)	Climatic praise to God	

Psalms

Classification: Poetry / Worship

Author: Primarily David; others include Asaph, Sons of Korah, Solomon, Moses

Date of Composition: 1000–400 B.C.

Historical Context: Israelite worship, national crises, and personal devotion over centuries.

Purpose and Theme

The Psalms provide prayers, praises, laments, and expressions of faith, forming Israel's primary liturgical literature.

Theme: Worship, prayer, and reflection on God's character.

Structure

- Book I (1–41), Book II (42–72), Book III (73–89), Book IV (90–106), Book V (107–150)

Key Scriptures

- Psalm 23:1 – "The LORD is my shepherd; I shall not want."
- Psalm 19:7 – "The law of the LORD is perfect."
- Psalm 51:10 – "Create in me a clean heart, O God."

Key Words / Concepts

- Worship
- Praise
- Lament
- Faithfulness of God

Major Figures

David, Asaph, Korahites, Solomon, Moses.

Timeline / Setting

Composition spans the monarchy and post-exilic period (~1000–400 B.C.).

Proverbs

Classification: Wisdom

Author: Solomon, Agur, Lemuel (traditionally)

Date of Composition: ca. 950–700 B.C.

Historical Context: Wisdom literature for moral, ethical, and spiritual instruction within Israel.

Purpose and Theme

Proverbs imparts practical wisdom for living in accordance with God's will, emphasizing moral discernment, righteousness, and the fear of the LORD.

Theme: The pursuit of wisdom as the foundation of life.

Key Scriptures

- Proverbs 1:7 – "The fear of the LORD is the beginning of knowledge."
- Proverbs 3:5–6 – "Trust in the LORD with all your heart."
- Proverbs 16:3 – Commit your works to the LORD.

Key Words / Concepts

- Wisdom (ḥokmah)
- Fear of the LORD
- Righteousness
- Discretion

Major Figures

Solomon, Agur, Lemuel, wise men of Israel.

Timeline / Setting

During the United Monarchy and post-Solomonic period (~950–700 B.C.).

Ecclesiastes

Classification: Wisdom / Philosophical

Author: Traditionally Solomon

Date of Composition: ca. 935 B.C.

Historical Context: Reflections on life, purpose, and human mortality after Solomon's reign.

Purpose and Theme

Ecclesiastes explores the vanity of human endeavors and the search for meaning, concluding that fulfillment is found in reverent obedience to God.

Theme: The futility of life without God.

Key Scriptures

- Ecclesiastes 1:2 – "Vanity of vanities, all is vanity."
- Ecclesiastes 12:13 – "Fear God and keep His commandments."

Key Words / Concepts

- Vanity (hebel)
- Wisdom
- Mortality
- Reverence

Major Figures

Solomon (as "Preacher" or Qoheleth).

Timeline / Setting

United Monarchy, late reign of Solomon (~935 B.C.).

Song of Solomon (Song of Songs)

Classification: Wisdom / Poetry

Author: Traditionally Solomon

Date of Composition: ca. 950–900 B.C.

Historical Context: Celebrates love, marriage, and covenantal relationship in poetic form.

Purpose and Theme

Song of Solomon portrays romantic love and marital intimacy as a reflection of God's love for His people. Often interpreted allegorically as God and Israel or Christ and the Church.

Theme: Love, desire, and covenantal relationship.

Key Scriptures

- Song 2:4 – "He brought me to the banqueting house."
- Song 8:6 – "Set me as a seal upon your heart."

Key Words / Concepts

- Love
- Intimacy
- Covenant
- Desire

Major Figures

The Beloved (male), the Shulammite (female), friends and chorus.

Timeline / Setting

United Monarchy (~950–900 B.C.), likely Solomon's court.

Summary of the Poetical and Wisdom Books (Job–Song of Solomon

Book	Theme	Date (B.C.)	Setting	Key Figures	Key Scripture
Job	Suffering and Divine Justice	2000–1000	Land of Uz	Job, Elihu	Job 19:25
Psalms	Worship and Praise	1000–400	Israel	David, Asaph	Psalm 23:1
Proverbs	Wisdom and Righteousness	950–700	Israel	Solomon, Agur	Prov 1:7
Ecclesiastes	Life's Meaning	935	Israel	Solomon	Eccl 12:13
Song of Solomon	Love and Covenant	950–900	Israel	Solomon, Shulammite	Song 8:6

Prophetic Books

The 400 Years of Silence Between the Old and New Testaments

Philosophies and Theories of the Intertestamental Era

The period between the Old and New Testaments—often referred to as the *400 Years of Silence*—marks a profound and transformative chapter in biblical history. Although no canonical Scripture was written during this time, it was far from spiritually inactive. The world of Judaism and the broader ancient world underwent significant philosophical, political, and religious shifts that set the stage for the coming of Christ and the rise of the New Testament Church.

The Role and Evolution of the Prophet

The Hebrew word for *prophet*, **nabi** (נָבִיא), derives from a root meaning "to bubble forth" or "to utter," implying someone who speaks by divine inspiration. A prophet was, quite literally, the *mouthpiece of God*—one who proclaimed His will and truth to the people.

> In earlier times, prophets were also called **seers**—*ro'eh* and *hozeh*—titles found in passages such as 1 Samuel 9:9 and 2 Samuel 24:11. These terms emphasize the visionary nature of the prophetic gift: the *seer* beheld divine revelation, while the *prophet* proclaimed it. Together, they served as God's direct communicators, making His will known to His people (cf. Exodus 7:1; Jeremiah 1:9; 2 Peter 1:20–21). Defining the Ministry of the Prophet The average dictionary defines a prophet as: 1. one who utters divinely inspired revelations; the writer of one of the prophetic books; one regarded by a group of followers as the final authoritative revealer of God's will; 2. one gifted with more than ordinary spiritual and moral insight; especially an inspired poet; 3. one who foretells future events: predictor; 4. an effective or leading spokesman for a cause, doctrine, or group; 5. a spiritual seer.

> The prophets were considered Holy men of God in particular, and in many ways, greater authorities than the priests. Ro'eh, "seer," from raa'ah "to see", was the term used in Samuel's time, commonly referred to as "beforetime". Nabiy' was the term as far back as the Pentateuch, while Ro'eh appeared as we said in Samuel's time. Chozeh "seer or gazer upon the Spirit realm," from the more poetic chazeh "see," is first found in, 2 Sam 24:11- Now when David arose in the morning, the word of the Lord came to the prophet Gad, David's seer, and is frequently used in the Chronicles. It came into use when ro'eh was becoming less used while the term nabi' was being resumed. Chazown is used in the Pentateuch, Samuel, Chronicles, Job, and the writings of the Old Testament prophets. It's the name used for prophetic revelation. It is suggested that this refers to the kings seer, seers such as Gad, David's seer, Iddo and Jehu, the son of Hanani during Solomon's kingship, and Asaph under Jehoshaphat (1 Chr. 29:30; 35:15 and Amos 7:12). Prophet in the Greek, means the interpreter, from profeemi, which means " to speak forth" truths for another, as in the case of Aaron being called as prophet to Moses (or his spokesman) expounding upon the will of God. In the scriptures they spoke the divinely inspired truths

of God beforehand unknown. Predicting is a leading function of the prophet, as in Deuteronomy 18:22; Jeremiah 28:9, Acts 2:30 and 1 Peter 1:10. (Vinnett, 2022)

Prophets Throughout Scripture

From the earliest days, individuals such as **Enoch**, **Abraham**, and **Moses** were considered prophets because they carried messages directly from God (Genesis 20:7; Deuteronomy 18:15; Hosea 12:13). Others, like **Miriam** (Exodus 15:20) and **Deborah** (Judges 4:4), were recognized as prophetesses, affirming that both men and women served as divine messengers.

During Samuel's time, the prophetic office became more structured. **Schools of the prophets** were established in places such as Ramah, Bethel, Gilgal, Gibeah, and Jericho (1 Samuel 19:18–24; 2 Kings 2:3, 15; 4:38). These institutions trained young men—known as the "sons of the prophets"—not only in the sacred arts of teaching and proclamation but also in moral integrity and devotion. Their mission was to uphold spiritual truth and act as a moral compass alongside the priesthood and monarchy.

The Prophets in Historical Context

The Old Testament canon includes the writings of sixteen prophets, traditionally grouped by their historical settings:

1. **Prophets of the Northern Kingdom (Israel):** Hosea, Amos, Joel, Jonah
2. **Prophets of Judah:** Isaiah, Jeremiah, Obadiah, Micah, Nahum, Habakkuk, Zephaniah
3. **Prophets of the Captivity:** Ezekiel, Daniel
4. **Prophets of the Restoration:** Haggai, Zechariah, Malachi

These are further categorized as **Major Prophets** (Isaiah, Jeremiah, Lamentations, Ezekiel, Daniel) and **Minor Prophets** (the remaining twelve), not by importance but by the length of their writings.

The Silence and the Shift

After Malachi, the prophetic voice grew silent. Yet during these four centuries, history did not stand still. Empires rose and fell—the Persians, Greeks, and Romans—each influencing the Jewish world in profound ways. The Hebrew Scriptures were translated into Greek (the Septuagint), synagogues emerged as centers of worship and study, and various philosophical movements such as **Stoicism**, **Epicureanism**, and **Hellenism** spread throughout the Mediterranean world.

These developments set the cultural and spiritual backdrop for the New Testament. The longing for a Messiah deepened, and prophetic expectation reached a fever pitch. When John the Baptist appeared proclaiming, "Repent, for the kingdom of heaven is at hand," it marked the end of the silence and the dawn of a new era of revelation (Matthew 3:1–3).

The Continuation of Prophecy in the New Testament

In the New Testament, prophecy found its ultimate fulfillment in **Jesus Christ**, the great Prophet and Son of God (Luke 24:19). He embodied and transcended all who came before Him, speaking not just *for* God, but *as* God incarnate.

The prophetic office continued in the early Church as well (1 Corinthians 12:28; Ephesians 2:20–21), where certain believers were empowered by the Holy Spirit to speak new revelations and strengthen the body of Christ. Unlike teachers, who explained established truths, prophets were used to declare divine insight and guidance for the growing Church.

Major Prophets

Isaiah

Classification: Major Prophet

Author: Isaiah

Date of Composition: ca. 740–680 B.C.

Historical Context: Kingdom of Judah threatened by Assyria; social injustice, idolatry, and international conflict.

Purpose and Theme

Isaiah addresses judgment and salvation, emphasizing God's holiness and the coming Messiah.

Theme: The sovereignty of God and the hope of redemption.

Key Scriptures

- Isaiah 6:8 – "Here am I; send me."
- Isaiah 7:14 – Virgin birth prophecy.
- Isaiah 53 – Suffering Servant.

Key Words / Concepts

- Holiness
- Judgment
- Messiah
- Salvation

Major Figures

Isaiah, Ahaz, Hezekiah.

Timeline / Setting

Judah, 8th century B.C., during Assyrian threat (c. 740–680 B.C.).

Jeremiah

Classification: Major Prophet

Author: Jeremiah

Date of Composition: ca. 627–580 B.C.

Historical Context: Judah facing Babylonian conquest and exile.

Purpose and Theme

Jeremiah warns of imminent judgment due to Israel's covenant unfaithfulness and foretells the new covenant.

Theme: Judgment, repentance, and hope for restoration.

Key Scriptures

- Jeremiah 1:5 – God's calling before birth.
- Jeremiah 31:31–34 – Promise of the New Covenant.

Key Words / Concepts

- Covenant
- Repentance
- Exile
- Restoration

Major Figures

Jeremiah, King Josiah, Zedekiah.

Timeline / Setting

Judah, late 7th to early 6th century B.C., leading to Babylonian exile (~627–586 B.C.).

Lamentations

Classification: Major Prophet / Poetic

Author: Traditionally Jeremiah

Date of Composition: ca. 586 B.C.

Historical Context: After the fall of Jerusalem to Babylon.

Purpose and Theme

Lamentations mourns the destruction of Jerusalem and the temple, emphasizing human grief and God's justice.

Theme: Sorrow, judgment, and hope in God's mercy.

Key Scriptures

- Lamentations 3:22–23 – "His mercies never come to an end."

Key Words / Concepts

- Lament
- Judgment
- Mercy

Major Figures

Jeremiah (author); Judahites in exile.

Timeline / Setting

Jerusalem, 586 B.C., post-destruction.

Ezekiel

Classification: Major Prophet

Author: Ezekiel

Date of Composition: ca. 593–571 B.C.

Historical Context: Babylonian exile; Israel's spiritual and physical destruction.

Purpose and Theme

Ezekiel calls Israel to repentance, emphasizes God's sovereignty, and foretells the restoration of the nation and temple.

Theme: Judgment and restoration under God's holiness.

Key Scriptures

- Ezekiel 36:26 – Promise of a new heart and spirit.
- Ezekiel 37 – Valley of dry bones (national restoration).

Key Words / Concepts

- Holiness
- Restoration
- Vision

Major Figures

Ezekiel, exiled Israelites.

Timeline / Setting

Babylon, 593–571 B.C., during exile.

Daniel

Classification: Major Prophet / Apocalyptic

Author: Daniel

Date of Composition: ca. 605–530 B.C.

Historical Context: Babylonian and Persian empires; Israel in exile.

Purpose and Theme

Daniel demonstrates God's sovereignty over nations, faithfulness in adversity, and prophetic visions of future kingdoms and the Messiah.

Theme: God's dominion and prophetic fulfillment.

Key Scriptures

- Daniel 2:44 – God's eternal kingdom.
- Daniel 6:26 – God's deliverance of the faithful.

Key Words / Concepts

- Prophecy
- Sovereignty
- Faithfulness
- Apocalypse

Major Figures

Daniel, Nebuchadnezzar, Darius, Belshazzar.

Timeline / Setting

Babylonian exile, 605–530 B.C.

Minor Prophets (The Twelve)

Hosea

Date: ca. 750–715 B.C.

Theme: God's covenantal love contrasted with Israel's unfaithfulness.

Key Scripture: Hosea 6:6 – "I desire mercy, not sacrifice."

Joel

Date: uncertain, possibly 835–796 B.C. or post-exilic

Theme: Day of the Lord; call to repentance.

Key Scripture: Joel 2:28 – Promise of the Spirit.

Amos

Date: ca. 760–750 B.C.

Theme: Social justice; God's judgment on Israel's corruption.

Key Scripture: Amos 5:24 – "Let justice roll down like waters."

Obadiah

Date: ca. 586 B.C.

Theme: Judgment against Edom.

Key Scripture: Obadiah 1:15 – "The day of the LORD is near."

Jonah

Date: ca. 780–750 B.C.

Theme: God's mercy extends to the nations; repentance is accepted.

Key Scripture: Jonah 2:2 – Prayer from the fish's belly.

Micah

Date: ca. 740–700 B.C.

Theme: Judgment and hope; prophecy of the Messiah from Bethlehem.

Key Scripture: Micah 5:2 – "From you shall come forth… a ruler in Israel."

Nahum

Date: ca. 663–612 B.C.

Theme: God's judgment on Nineveh; justice against oppression.

Key Scripture: Nahum 1:7 – God is good and refuge in trouble.

Habakkuk

Date: ca. 612–589 B.C.

Theme: God's justice; faith in divine timing.

Key Scripture: Habakkuk 2:4 – "The righteous shall live by faith."

Zephaniah

Date: ca. 640–609 B.C.

Theme: Day of the Lord; call to repentance and hope.

Key Scripture: Zephaniah 3:17 – God rejoices over His people.

Haggai

Date: 520 B.C.

Theme: Rebuilding the temple; obedience to God's call.

Key Scripture: Haggai 1:7–8 – "Consider your ways."

Zechariah

Date: 520–518 B.C.

Theme: Encouragement to rebuild the temple; Messianic visions.

Key Scripture: Zechariah 9:9 – Prophecy of the coming King on a donkey.

Malachi

Date: ca. 450–400 B.C.

Theme: Faithfulness in worship; promise of the coming messenger.

Key Scripture: Malachi 3:1 – "Behold, I send my messenger…"

Summary of the Prophetic Books (Isaiah–Malachi)

Book	Theme	Date (B.C.)	Setting	Key Figures	Key Scripture
Isaiah	Judgment & Salvation	740-680	Judah	Isaiah, Hezekiah	Isa 53
Jeremiah	Covenant & Exile	627-580	Judah	Jeremiah, Josiah	Jer 31:31-34
Lamentations	Mourning & Hope	586	Jerusalem	Jeremiah	Lam 3:22-23
Ezekiel	Holiness & Restoration	593-571	Babylon	Ezekiel	Ezek 37
Daniel	Sovereignty & Prophecy	605-530	Babylon	Daniel	Dan 2:44
Hosea	Covenant Faithfulness	750-715	Israel	Hosea	Hos 6:6
Joel	Day of the Lord	835-796	Judah	Joel	Joel 2:28

Amos	Justice & Judgment	760-750	Israel	Amos	Amos 5:24
Obadiah	Judgment on Edom	586	Edom	Obadiah	Obad 1:15
Jonah	Repentance & Mercy	780-750	Nineveh	Jonah	Jonah 2:2
Micah	Judgment & Messiah	740-700	Judah	Micah	

The Old Covenant vs. The New Covenant

To understand your covenant as a Christian, recognize it as the New Covenant, established by Jesus' death and resurrection, which replaces older covenants. You enter this covenant through faith in Christ, repentance, baptism, and obedience. Knowing your covenant involves studying the Bible to understand its promises (like forgiveness of sins and a righteous identity), benefits (like peace and freedom from fear), and terms (faith and obedience).

What is the Christian Covenant?

- **A New and Binding Relationship:** It is a sacred, binding promise between God and believers, establishing a deep relationship and a path to salvation.
- **Sealed by Christ's Sacrifice:** The New Covenant is sealed by the blood of Jesus, which cleanses believers from sin and provides access to God's grace.
- **An Act of Grace:** God initiates the covenant, inviting people to join Him through His unmerited favor.

How to Enter and Maintain the Covenant

1. **Faith and Repentance:** Believe in God and Jesus Christ, and repent of your sins.
2. **Confession and Baptism:** Confess your sins and be baptized to signify your commitment.
3. **Obedience:** Live a life of obedience to God's commandments.
4. **Study the Word:** Regularly read and meditate on the Bible to understand your covenant rights and promises.
5. **Maintain the Relationship:** Just as any relationship needs nurturing, you must continually invest in your covenant relationship through prayer, learning, and love for God.

Benefits of Knowing Your Covenant

- **Spiritual Identity:** You receive God's laws in your heart and mind and are made righteous through Christ.
- **Freedom from Fear:** Knowledge of your covenant rights brings peace, as you learn to rely on God's provision rather than anxiety.
- **Victory in Spiritual Battles:** Understanding the privileges of the covenant equips you for spiritual warfare and helps you overcome challenges.
- **Abundant Life:** It unlocks the blessings and abundant life that Jesus' sacrifice purchased for those who believe.

I. The Old Covenant – The Law and Sacrifice

Established between God and Israel through Moses at Mount Sinai (Exodus 19–24). Based on obedience to God's Law and confirmed through animal sacrifices.
- Revealed God's holiness and the seriousness of sin.
- Set Israel apart as God's chosen people.
- Foreshadowed the coming of a perfect Savior.
Limitations: Could not change the human heart and required continuous sacrifices for sin.

II. The New Covenant – Grace and Redemption

Fulfilled through Jesus Christ and established by His death and resurrection (Luke 22:20).
- Internal transformation: God's Spirit changes hearts, not just behavior.
- Permanent forgiveness: Jesus' one-time sacrifice covers all sin (Hebrews 10:10–14).
- Direct access to God: Jesus is our mediator (1 Timothy 2:5).
- Universal invitation: Open to all people, not just Israel (John 3:16).

Comparison Chart

Aspect	Old Covenant	New Covenant
Mediator	Moses	Jesus Christ
Law Written On	Stone tablets	Hearts
Sacrifice	Repeated animal offerings	One perfect sacrifice
Access to God	Through priests	Direct through Christ
Sign	Circumcision, Sabbath	Communion (Lord's Supper)
Basis	Obedience to the Law	Faith in Christ
Power Source	Human effort	Holy Spirit
Result	Condemnation for sin	Forgiveness and grace

IV. Why the New Covenant Matters Today

1. We live under grace, not law (Romans 6:14).
2. We are empowered, not enslaved (Romans 8:1–4).
3. We walk in relationship, not religion.

Closing Thought

The Old Covenant pointed to what was coming — the need for a Savior. The New Covenant fulfilled that promise — bringing forgiveness, freedom, and fellowship with God.
Hebrews 8:6 – 'But in fact the ministry Jesus has received is as superior to theirs as the covenant of which he is mediator is superior to the old one, since the new covenant is established on better promises.'

New Testament

The New Testament was written primarily to **record, explain, and spread the message of Jesus Christ** and the early Christian faith. It served multiple purposes:

1. **Preserve the Life and Teachings of Jesus** – The Gospels (Matthew, Mark, Luke, John) were written to document Jesus' birth, ministry, miracles, death, and resurrection so that future generations could know the truth about Him.
2. **Provide Guidance to Early Christians** – Letters (Epistles) written by apostles like Paul, Peter, James, John, and others gave instruction, encouragement, and correction to churches and believers facing persecution, moral challenges, or doctrinal confusion.
3. **Explain Salvation and God's Plan** – The New Testament clarifies how Jesus fulfills Old Testament prophecy, how faith in Him leads to salvation, and how believers are to live in relationship with God.
4. **Encourage Hope and Endurance** – Books like Revelation and the Epistles address the ultimate victory of God, the coming judgment, and the hope of eternal life, motivating believers to persevere through trials.
5. **Unify the Early Church** – By providing authoritative teaching and shared texts, the New Testament helped maintain doctrinal consistency and community identity among diverse early Christian groups.

In short, it was written to **teach, correct, encourage, and preserve the message of Christ** for both the first-century church and all subsequent generations.

Organization of the New Testament

Matthew Mark Luke John	**GOSPELS**
Acts	**HISTORY**
Romans 1 & 2 Corinthians Galatians Ephesians Philippians Colossians 1 & 2 Thessalonians 1 & 2 Timothy Titus Philemon Hebrews James 1 & 2 Peter 1, 2 &3 John	**EPISTLES**
Revelation	**PROPHECY**

The Gospels

The gospels are documentation of the saving work of God through his Son Jesus Christ. The books included in the gospels are Matthew, Mark, Luke and John. The gospels were written to record the works of Christ. They introduce Christ to a new community of believers and lastly to guard against heresy. The foundation of the synoptic gospels is found in Isaiah 52:7

How beautiful upon the mountains
Are the feet of him who brings good news,
Who proclaims peace,
Who brings glad tidings of good *things*,
Who proclaims salvation,
Who says to Zion,
"Your God reigns!"

Synoptic Gospels

The term Synoptic Gospels was coined by Johannes Griesbach in 1783 to describe the very similar pictures of Jesus portrayed in Matthew, Mark, Luke. It comes from the Greek terms that means "with one eye" or at the same time. The Bible's four gospels paint four portraits of Jesus. While each gospel follows Christ on the same journey, they each describe the journey a little differently.

The uncertain relationship between the synoptic gospels is known as "the synoptic problem." The main question of the synoptic problem is: hypothesis best accounts for the combination of exact agreement and wide divergence that characterizes the 3 gospels? The thought shared between historians and theologians alike is that Matthew, Mark, and Luke share a source or sources of some kind.

An example of passages that cause them to agree on this point:

For example, take a look at these passages where Jesus interacts with little children:

Matthew 19:13–14	Mark 10:13–14	Luke 18:15–16
"Then little children were brought to Jesus for him to place his hands on them and pray for them. But the disciples rebuked those who brought them. Jesus said, 'Let the little children come to me, and do not hinder them, for the kingdom of heaven belongs to such as these.'"	"People were bringing little children to Jesus to have him touch them, but the disciples rebuked them. When Jesus saw this, he was indignant. He said to them, 'Let the little children come to me, and do not hinder them, for the kingdom of God belongs to such as these.'"	"People were also bringing babies to Jesus to have him touch them. When the disciples saw this, they rebuked them. But Jesus called the children to him and said, 'Let the little children come to me, and do not hinder them, for the kingdom of God belongs to such as these.'"

The quote from Jesus is identical in all three passages, the text prior to the listen quotes has slightly different wording, but say the same thing.

Life of Jesus

Infancy narrative
Flight to Egypt
Dedication at the temple
Jesus in the temple
Matthew 1:2-2:23; Luke 1:5-2:52

Jesus baptism
Temptation
Matthew 3:1-4:11; Mark 1:2-13; Luke 3:1-4:13; John 1:19-34

Wedding at Cana
First Journey to Jerusalem (Passover, John 2:13)
Discourse with Nicodemus
John 2-3

Discourse with the woman of Samaria
Sermon on the Mount/Sermon on the Plain
Matthew 4:12-7:29; Mark 3:19b-7:23; Luke 4:14-6:49 John 4:1-46
Matthew 8:1-15:20; Mark 3:19b-7:23 Luke 7:1-9:17; John 4:46b-6:59

The Nicene Council

The **First Council of Nicaea**, was a major gathering of Christian bishops held in **A.D. 325** in the city of **Nicaea** (modern-day İznik, Turkey). It was the **first ecumenical council** (meaning worldwide or universal council) of the Christian Church and marked a defining moment in early Christian history.

Here's a breakdown of its key points:

Background
- The Roman Emperor **Constantine the Great** called the council after Christianity was legalized through the **Edict of Milan (A.D. 313)**.
- The Church was facing internal division, especially over the teachings of a priest named **Arius**, who claimed that **Jesus Christ was not fully divine** but a created being.
- This controversy, known as the **Arian controversy**, threatened to divide the Church.

Main Purpose
- To **settle the dispute about the nature of Christ**—specifically, whether Jesus was of the same substance as God the Father or a lesser, created being.

Major Decisions and Outcomes
1. **The Nicene Creed:**
   - The council produced a formal statement of Christian belief known as the **Nicene Creed**.
   - It declared that Jesus Christ is **"of one substance (homoousios) with the Father,"** affirming His full divinity.
2. **Condemnation of Arianism:**
   - Arius and his teachings were declared **heretical**, and his writings were ordered to be burned.
3. **Easter Date:**
   - The council also established a **uniform date for celebrating Easter**, separate from the Jewish Passover.
4. **Church Order and Discipline:**
   - The council discussed various issues of **church governance**, **the role of bishops**, and **disciplinary matters** among clergy.

Legacy
- The Nicene Council **unified Christian doctrine** and helped establish **orthodox Trinitarian theology**—the belief in one God in three persons: Father, Son, and Holy Spirit.
- It set the precedent for future **ecumenical councils** that would continue to shape Christian doctrine.
- The **Nicene Creed** remains a central statement of faith in many Christian denominations today, including Catholic, Orthodox, and many Protestant churches.

Matthew

Classification: Gospel (Synoptic)

Author: Matthew (Levi), a former tax collector and one of the Twelve Apostles

Date of Composition: ca. A.D. 60–65

Audience: Jewish Christians

Purpose and Theme

Matthew presents Jesus as the Messiah and King, the fulfillment of Old Testament prophecy.

Theme: Jesus is the promised King of the Jews and fulfillment of the Law and Prophets.

Structure

1. Birth and Preparation of the Messiah (Chs. 1–4)
2. Teachings of the Messiah (Sermon on the Mount, Chs. 5–7)
3. Kingdom Miracles and Parables (Chs. 8–25)
4. Death and Resurrection (Chs. 26–28)

Key Scriptures

- Matthew 5:17 – "I came not to abolish the Law but to fulfill it."
- Matthew 28:19–20 – The Great Commission.

Key Words / Concepts

- Kingdom of Heaven
- Fulfillment
- Messiah

Major Figures

Jesus, John the Baptist, Peter, the Twelve Disciples, Pilate.

Timeline / Setting

Ministry of Jesus, ca. A.D. 27–30, primarily in Judea and Galilee.

Mark

Classification: Gospel (Synoptic)

Author: John Mark, companion of Peter

Date of Composition: ca. A.D. 55–60

Audience: Roman Christians

Purpose and Theme

Mark portrays Jesus as the Servant of God who acts with power and compassion.

Theme: Jesus is the suffering yet triumphant Servant.

Structure

1. Ministry of John and Baptism of Jesus (1)
2. Galilean Ministry (2–9)
3. Journey to Jerusalem (10–11)
4. Passion and Resurrection (14–16)

Key Scriptures

- Mark 10:45 – "The Son of Man came not to be served but to serve."
- Mark 16:6 – "He has risen."

Key Words / Concepts

- Immediately
- Servanthood
- Power

Major Figures

Jesus, Peter, James, John, the Twelve.

Timeline / Setting

Jesus' ministry (~A.D. 27–30), written from Rome.

Luke

Classification: Gospel (Synoptic)

Author: Luke the physician, companion of Paul

Date of Composition: ca. A.D. 60–62

Audience: Gentile Christians (esp. Theophilus)

Purpose and Theme

Luke presents Jesus as the Son of Man, emphasizing His humanity and compassion for all people.

Theme: Jesus brings salvation to all humanity.

Structure

1. Birth and Preparation (1–4)
2. Ministry in Galilee and Judea (5–19)
3. Passion and Resurrection (20–24)

Key Scriptures

- Luke 19:10 – "The Son of Man came to seek and save the lost."
- Luke 24:49 – Promise of the Spirit.

Key Words / Concepts

- Son of Man
- Compassion
- Salvation

Major Figures

Jesus, Mary, John the Baptist, Peter, Pilate, the disciples.

Timeline / Setting

A.D. 27–30; written from Greece or Rome.

John

Classification: Gospel

Author: Apostle John

Date of Composition: ca. A.D. 85–90

Audience: General (emphasis on universal belief)

Purpose and Theme

John focuses on Jesus' divine identity as the Son of God, aiming to inspire belief for eternal life.

Theme: Jesus is the eternal Word made flesh.

Structure

1. Prologue (1:1–18)
2. Signs and Discourses (2–12)
3. Farewell and Passion (13–20)
4. Epilogue (21)

Key Scriptures

- John 1:1 – "In the beginning was the Word."
- John 3:16 – "For God so loved the world."
- John 20:31 – Purpose statement.

Key Words / Concepts

- Believe
- Life
- Light
- Word (Logos)

Major Figures

Jesus, John the Baptist, Nicodemus, Mary Magdalene, Thomas, Peter.

Timeline / Setting

Jesus' ministry (~A.D. 27–30); written from Ephesus.

Historical Book

Acts of the Apostles

Classification: Historical Narrative

Author: Luke

Date of Composition: ca. A.D. 63–70

Audience: Theophilus / Early Church

Purpose and Theme

Acts records the spread of the gospel from Jerusalem to Rome through the power of the Holy Spirit.

Theme: Empowerment of the Church through the Holy Spirit to fulfill Christ's mission.

Structure

1. Birth of the Church (1–7)
2. Expansion to Judea and Samaria (8–12)
3. Paul's Missionary Journeys (13–28)

Key Scriptures

- Acts 1:8 – "You will receive power when the Holy Spirit has come upon you."
- Acts 2:38 – Peter's call to repentance.

Key Words / Concepts

- Holy Spirit
- Witness
- Church

Major Figures

Peter, Paul, Stephen, Philip, Barnabas, James.

Timeline / Setting

Events A.D. 30–62; written from Rome.

Main Purposes of the Book of Acts
- **Church History:**
    - Chronicles the founding and growth of the early church.
    - Shows the spread of the gospel and establishment of congregations.
    - Demonstrates the work of the risen Lord and the Holy Spirit through the apostles.
- **Defense of the Faith:**
    - Records Christian defenses to Jews and Gentiles (e.g., 4:8–12; 25:8–11).
    - Illustrates how the early church navigated cultural, religious, and political challenges.
    - Likely served as a record for Paul's defense while awaiting trial in Rome.
- **Guidance for the Church:**
    - Provides principles applied to real situations, including persecution and challenges.
    - Remains a practical guide for the church until Christ returns.
- **Triumph Over Persecution:**
    - Shows the gospel's spread from Jerusalem to Rome and beyond.
    - Highlights the church's success as a work of Christ and the Holy Spirit, not merely human effort.

The Ministry of the Holy Spirit

The **Holy Spirit** is the third Person of the Trinity—fully God, coequal with the Father and the Son. His ministry involves empowering, guiding, teaching, convicting, and transforming believers and the Church.

Key Aspects of the Holy Spirit's Ministry
1. Regeneration (New Birth)
- The Holy Spirit gives spiritual life to believers.
- **Key Scripture:** John 3:5-6; Titus 3:5

2. Indwelling
- He permanently lives within believers from the moment of salvation.
- **Key Scripture:** 1 Corinthians 6:19; Romans 8:11

3. Seal and Guarantee
- The Spirit seals believers, marking them as God's, and guaranteeing their future redemption.
- **Key Scripture:** Ephesians 1:13-14; 2 Corinthians 1:22

4. Empowerment for Service
- The Holy Spirit equips believers for ministry through spiritual gifts.
- **Key Scripture:** Acts 1:8; 1 Corinthians 12:4-11

5. Conviction of Sin
- He convicts the world of sin, righteousness, and judgment.
- **Key Scripture:** John 16:8

6. Guidance into Truth
- The Spirit leads believers, helping them understand and apply God's Word.
- **Key Scripture:** John 16:13; Romans 8:14

7. Sanctification
- The Spirit transforms believers into the image of Christ by producing spiritual fruit.
- **Key Scripture:** Galatians 5:22-23; 2 Thessalonians 2:13

8. Intercession
- The Holy Spirit intercedes for believers in prayer.
- **Key Scripture:** Romans 8:26-27

9. Fellowship
- He creates unity in the Body of Christ and fosters spiritual community.
- **Key Scripture:** 2 Corinthians 13:14; Ephesians 4:3

Fruit of the Spirit
The visible evidence of the Spirit's work in a believer's life is seen in the **Fruit of the Spirit**:
- Love, Joy, Peace, Patience, Kindness, Goodness, Faithfulness, Gentleness, Self-control (Galatians 5:22-23)

Gifts of the Spirit
The Holy Spirit gives spiritual gifts for the edification of the Church. Examples:
- Teaching, prophecy, healing, administration, tongues, wisdom, and more (1 Corinthians 12; Romans 12; Ephesians 4)

Symbols of the Holy Spirit in Scripture
- **Dove** — Peace and purity (Matthew 3:16)
- **Wind** — Invisible power (John 3:8; Acts 2:2)
- **Fire** — Purification and presence (Acts 2:3)
- **Oil** — Anointing and consecration (1 Samuel 16:13)

Key Ministries of the Holy Spirit

Ministry	Description	Key Scripture
Regeneration	Gives new spiritual life (born again)	John 3:5-6; Titus 3:5
Indwelling	Lives within every believer permanently	1 Corinthians 6:19; Romans 8:11
Seal and Guarantee	Marks believers as God's own and assures future redemption	Ephesians 1:13-14; 2 Corinthians 1:22
Empowerment	Enables believers for ministry and witness	Acts 1:8; 1 Corinthians 12:4-11
Conviction of Sin	Reveals sin and need for salvation	John 16:8
Guidance into Truth	Shows God's will through Scripture and inward direction	John 16:13; Romans 8:14
Sanctification	Transforms believers into Christ's image	Galatians 5:22-23; 2 Thessalonians 2:13
Intercession	Prays for us when we don't know how to pray	Romans 8:26-27
Fellowship	Creates spiritual unity among believers	2 Corinthians 13:14; Ephesians 4:3

Ministry of the Holy Spirit
I. Introduction to the Holy Spirit
- Personhood of the Spirit
- Third Person of the Trinity

II. The Saving Work of the Holy Spirit
1. **Conviction of Sin** – John 16:8
   - Reveals sin to bring repentance
2. **Regeneration** – John 3:5-6
   - New birth through the Spirit

III. The Indwelling and Sealing Work
1. **Indwelling Presence** – 1 Corinthians 6:19
   - Every believer becomes a temple of the Spirit
2. **Seal and Guarantee of Redemption** – Ephesians 1:13-14
   - Assurance of salvation

IV. Empowering for Christian Living
1. **Spiritual Gifts** – 1 Corinthians 12
   - Empowerment for ministry
2. **Fruit of the Spirit** – Galatians 5:22-23
   - Evidence of spiritual growth

V. Guiding the Believer
- Teaching and leading in truth – John 16:13
- Personal and corporate direction – Romans 8:14

VI. The Spirit's Role in Prayer
- Interceding when we don't know what to pray – Romans 8:26-27

VII. Unifying the Body of Christ
- Creates oneness and unity – Ephesians 4:3

VIII. Symbols of the Holy Spirit
- Dove, Fire, Wind, Oil, Water

IX. Conclusion
- The Holy Spirit is active in every part of the believer's life
- A call to walk in the Spirit daily – Galatians 5:25

Epistles

The term **"epistle"** comes from the Greek word *epistole*, which simply means **"a letter."** Most of the New Testament epistles are attributed to the Apostle Paul. Specifically:

- **Paul** wrote 13 letters.
- **John** wrote 3 letters.
- **Peter** wrote 2 letters.
- **James** and **Jude** each wrote 1 letter.
- **Hebrews** is included among the epistles but its author is unknown.

The epistles are commonly categorized into four groups: **Pauline, General, Prison, and Pastoral**.

Pauline Epistles	General Epistles	Prison Epistles	Pastoral Epistles
Romans I Corinthians II Corinthians Galatians Ephesians Philippians Colossians I Thessalonians II Thessalonians I Timothy II Timothy Titus Philemon	Hebrews James I Peter II Peter I John II John III John Jude	Ephesians Philippians Colossians Philemon	I Timothy II Timothy Titus

Pauline Epistles

Tamiya D. Lewis

Why was the Apostle Paul Chosen

The Apostle Paul played a unique and powerful role in the early Church, and there are both spiritual and practical reasons why he wrote most of the New Testament.

1. God's Divine Choice

Paul was personally chosen by Jesus Christ to be His messenger.

- On the road to Damascus (Acts 9:1–19), Jesus appeared to Paul in a bright light and called him to turn from persecuting Christians to preaching the Gospel.

- Jesus said:
  "He is a chosen instrument of Mine to carry My name before the Gentiles and kings and the children of Israel."
  — Acts 9:15 (ESV)

Paul's calling was divinely appointed, showing that God can use anyone—even a former persecutor—to spread His truth.

2. His Mission to the Gentiles

Paul was specially chosen to bring the message of Christ to the Gentiles (non-Jews).

- While other apostles mainly focused on the Jews, Paul's ministry reached far beyond Israel—to Asia Minor, Greece, and Rome.

- Because of this broad mission, he wrote letters (Epistles) to many new churches and believers across the Roman Empire, explaining faith, salvation, and Christian living.

3. His Education and Background

Paul was highly educated in Jewish law under the famous teacher Gamaliel (Acts 22:3) and also a Roman citizen—which gave him access to both Jewish and Greco-Roman audiences.

- His training allowed him to bridge cultures and explain deep theological truths with clarity and authority.

- God used Paul's intelligence, logic, and writing skills to communicate the Gospel in a way that shaped Christian theology for centuries.

4. His Deep Spiritual Revelation

After his conversion, Paul received direct revelation from Jesus Christ (Galatians 1:11–12).

- The Holy Spirit guided his writing, making his letters not just personal messages but inspired Scripture.
- His epistles reveal profound truths about grace, faith, justification, and the Church—core foundations of Christian doctrine.

5. His Pastoral Heart

Paul's letters were written out of love and concern for the believers he had taught.

- He corrected false teachings, encouraged struggling churches, and gave practical instructions for Christian living.
- His writings continue to teach, correct, and strengthen believers today (2 Timothy 3:16–17).

Summary

Reason	Explanation
Divine Appointment	God personally chose Paul as His instrument.
Mission to Gentiles	Paul's wide travels required written instruction.
Strong Education	Paul's background equipped him to explain deep truths.
Spiritual Revelation	His writings were inspired by the Holy Spirit.
Pastoral Care	He wrote to guide, encourage, and correct the Church.

Romans

Date: ca. A.D. 57

Theme: Justification by faith and righteousness of God.

Key Scripture: Romans 1:16–17 – "The just shall live by faith."

Key Words: Righteousness, Faith, Grace.

Figures: Paul, Phoebe.

Setting: Written from Corinth.

1 Corinthians

Date: ca. A.D. 55

Theme: Unity, holiness, and order in the church.

Key Scripture: 1 Cor. 13:13 – "The greatest of these is love."

Key Words: Love, Spiritual gifts, Resurrection.

Figures: Paul, Apollos, Chloe's household.

Setting: Corinthian church issues.

2 Corinthians

Date: A.D. 56

Theme: Apostolic authority, suffering, and comfort in ministry.

Key Scripture: 2 Cor. 5:17 – "If anyone is in Christ, he is a new creation."

Key Words: Comfort, Reconciliation, Weakness.

1 Thessalonians

Date: A.D. 50–51

Theme: Hope in Christ's return.

Key Scripture: 1 Thess. 4:16–17 – The rapture.

Key Words: Hope, Encouragement, Coming of the Lord.

2 Thessalonians

Date: A.D. 51–52

Theme: Perseverance amid persecution; clarification of Christ's return.

Key Scripture: 2 Thess. 2:15 – Stand firm in the teachings.

Philemon

Date: A.D. 60–61

Theme: Forgiveness and Christian brotherhood.

Key Scripture: Philemon 1:16 – "No longer a slave, but a beloved brother."

General Epistles

Hebrews

Date: ca. A.D. 64–68

Theme: Superiority of Christ's priesthood and covenant.

Key Scripture: Heb. 4:14–16 – Our great High Priest.

Key Words: Better, Faith, Covenant.

James

Date: A.D. 45–50

Theme: Faith demonstrated through works.

Key Scripture: James 2:17 – "Faith without works is dead."

Key Words: Faith, Wisdom, Endurance.

1 Peter

Date: A.D. 63–64

Theme: Suffering for Christ and living hope.

Key Scripture: 1 Pet. 1:3–9 – Hope of resurrection.

2 Peter

Date: A.D. 65–68

Theme: Warning against false teachers; assurance of the Lord's return.

Key Scripture: 2 Pet. 3:9 – God's patience leads to repentance.

1 John

Date: A.D. 85–95

Theme: Assurance of salvation and love as proof of faith.

Key Scripture: 1 John 4:8 – "God is love."

2 John

Date: A.D. 90–95

Theme: Truth and love in the Christian walk.

Key Scripture: 2 John 1:6 – Walk in love and obedience.

3 John

Date: A.D. 90–95

Theme: Hospitality and faithfulness to truth.

Key Scripture: 3 John 1:4 – "I have no greater joy than to hear my children walk in truth."

Jude

Date: A.D. 65–80

Theme: Contend for the faith against false teachers.

Key Scripture: Jude 1:3 – "Contend earnestly for the faith."

Pastoral Epistles

1 Timothy

Date: A.D. 63–65

Theme: Church leadership and sound doctrine.

Key Scripture: 1 Tim. 4:12 – Example in speech and purity.

2 Timothy

Date: A.D. 66–67

Theme: Faithfulness in ministry despite hardship.

Key Scripture: 2 Tim. 4:7 – "I have fought the good fight."

Titus

Date: A.D. 63–65

Theme: Order and good works in the church.

Key Scripture: Titus 2:11–13 – Grace teaches us to live godly lives.

Apostle Paul's Ministry Journey

Journey / Phase	Approx. Date	Key Locations	Major Events & Ministry Highlights	Scripture References	Companions / Notes
Conversion & Early Ministry	AD 33–46	Damascus, Arabia, Jerusalem, Tarsus, Antioch	- Conversion on the road to Damascus - Baptized by Ananias - Begins preaching Jesus as the Son of God - Time in Arabia and return to Damascus - Fleeing Damascus - First visit to Jerusalem - Ministry in Tarsus and Antioch	Acts 9:1–31; Galatians 1:15–24	Barnabas (introduced Paul to apostles), Ananias
First Missionary Journey	AD 46–48	Antioch (Syria), Cyprus, Perga, Pisidian Antioch, Iconium, Lystra, Derbe	- Sent out by the Holy Spirit from Antioch - Preaches in synagogues - Faces opposition and persecution - Heals a crippled man in Lystra - Establishes churches in Galatia region - Returns to	Acts 13–14	Barnabas, John Mark (left early)

			Antioch to report results		
Jerusalem Council	AD 49	Jerusalem	- Debate over circumcision and Gentile believers - Decision: Gentiles not required to keep full Mosaic Law	Acts 15:1–35	Peter, James, Barnabas
Second Missionary Journey	AD 49–52	Antioch, Syria, Cilicia, Derbe, Lystra, Troas, Philippi, Thessalonica, Berea, Athens, Corinth, Ephesus	- Revisits churches - Adds Timothy to ministry team - Vision of the "Man of Macedonia" → Europe - Imprisoned in Philippi (with Silas) - Preaches in Athens (Mars Hill) - 18-month ministry in Corinth	Acts 15:36–18:22; 1 Thessalonians; 2 Thessalonians	Silas, Timothy, Luke, Priscilla & Aquila
Third Missionary Journey	AD 53–57	Galatia, Phrygia, Ephesus, Macedonia, Corinth, Troas, Miletus, Jerusalem	- Strengthens existing churches - Three-year ministry in Ephesus (miracles, revival, riots) - Writes several epistles (1 & 2 Corinthians, Romans)	Acts 18:23–21:17; 1 & 2 Corinthians; Romans	Timothy, Titus, Luke, others

			- Farewell to Ephesian elders at Miletus		
Arrest and Trials	AD 57–59	Jerusalem, Caesarea	- Arrested in Jerusalem - Speaks before Sanhedrin - Transferred to Caesarea - Trials before Felix, Festus, and Agrippa	Acts 21:27–26:32	Roman guards, Festus, Agrippa
Journey to Rome (Imprisonment)	AD 59–60	Caesarea → Sidon → Myra → Crete → Malta → Rome	- Appeals to Caesar - Survives shipwreck on Malta - Heals people on the island - Arrives in Rome under house arrest	Acts 27–28	Luke, Aristarchus
First Roman Imprisonment	AD 60–62	Rome	- Writes "Prison Epistles": Ephesians, Philippians, Colossians, Philemon - Continues preaching under house arrest	Acts 28:16–31; Eph., Phil., Col., Philem.	Epaphroditus, Onesimus, Timothy
Possible Fourth Journey (Post-Release)	AD 63–67	Crete, Ephesus, Macedonia, Nicopolis, Troas	- Possible missions after release - Writes pastoral letters (1 Timothy, Titus)	1 Tim.; Titus	Timothy, Titus

| Final Imprisonment and Martyrdom | AD 67–68 | Rome | - Writes final letter (2 Timothy)
- Executed under Nero (beheaded) | 2 Timothy | Luke ("Only Luke is with me") |

Summary Overview

Category	Details
Total Missionary Journeys	3 major journeys + possible 4th (after first imprisonment)
Primary Sending Church	Antioch of Syria
Major Themes in Ministry	Grace through faith, unity of Jew and Gentile, perseverance through suffering, spiritual maturity
Key Epistles	Romans, Corinthians, Galatians, Ephesians, Philippians, Colossians, Thessalonians, Timothy, Titus, Philemon
Death	Martyred in Rome (c. AD 67–68) under Emperor Nero

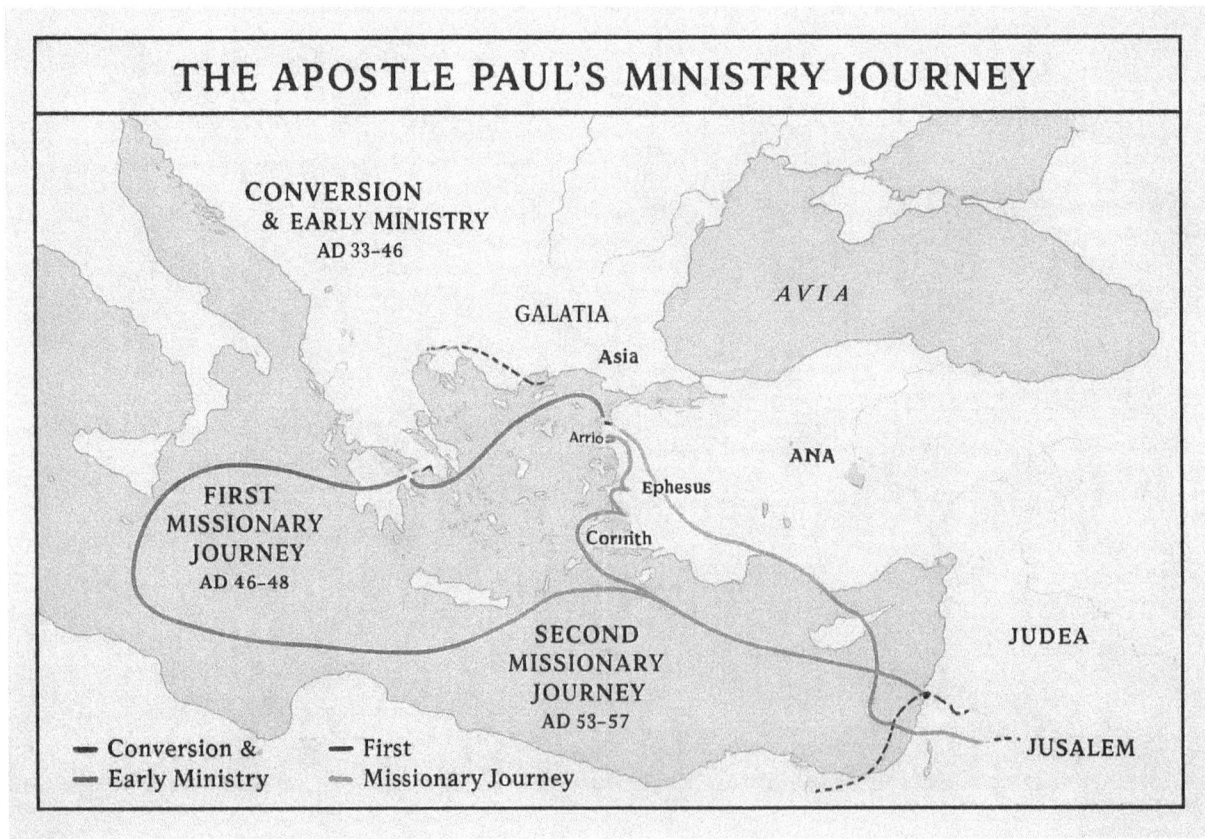

Apocalyptic Book

Revelation

Classification: Prophetic / Apocalyptic
Author: Apostle John
Date of Composition: ca. A.D. 95
Historical Context: Persecution under Emperor Domitian; written from Patmos.

Purpose and Theme

Revelation unveils the final victory of Christ, the judgment of evil, and the establishment of God's eternal kingdom.
Theme: Christ triumphant over evil and the ultimate renewal of creation.

Structure
1. Letters to the Seven Churches (Chs. 1–3)
2. Heavenly Visions and Judgments (Chs. 4–19)
3. Millennium and New Jerusalem (Chs. 20–22)

Key Scriptures
- Revelation 1:8 – "I am the Alpha and the Omega."
- Revelation 21:4 – "He will wipe away every tear."

Key Words / Concepts
- Victory
- Kingdom
- Judgment
- Worship

Major Figures
Jesus Christ (the Lamb), John, the Seven Churches, the Beast, the Bride.

Timeline / Setting
End of the first century, A.D. 95; prophetic scope: present, future, and eternal.

Summary of the New Testament Books

Book	Theme	Date (A.D.)	Author	Key Word	Key Scripture
Matthew	Messiah-King	60–65	Matthew	Fulfillment	Matt. 28:19–20
Mark	Servant of God	55–60	Mark	Immediately	Mark 10:45
Luke	Son of Man	60–62	Luke	Salvation	Luke 19:10
John	Son of God	85–90	John	Believe	John 3:16
Acts	Empowered Church	63–70	Luke	Spirit	Acts 1:8
Romans	Righteousness of God	57	Paul	Faith	Rom. 1:17
1 Corinthians	Church Order	55	Paul	Love	1 Cor. 13
2 Corinthians	Suffering & Comfort	56	Paul	Reconciliation	2 Cor. 5:17
Galatians	Freedom in Christ	48	Paul	Grace	Gal. 2:20
Ephesians	Unity in Christ	60–62	Paul	Body	Eph. 2:8
Philippians	Joy in Christ	61–62	Paul	Joy	Phil. 4:13
Colossians	Supremacy of Christ	60–61	Paul	Preeminence	Col. 1:15
1 & 2 Thess.	Hope in Christ's Return	50–52	Paul	Hope	1 Thess. 4:16
1 & 2 Timothy	Sound Doctrine	63–67	Paul	Faithfulness	2 Tim. 4:7
Titus	Good Works	63–65	Paul	Order	Titus 2:11
Philemon	Forgiveness	60–61	Paul	Brotherhood	Philem. 1:16
Hebrews	Superiority of Christ	64–68	Unknown	Better	Heb. 4:14
James	Faith and Works	45–50	James	Works	James 2:17
1 & 2 Peter	Hope and Warning	63–68	Peter	Suffering	1 Pet. 1:3
1–3 John	Love and Truth	85–95	John	Love	1 John 4:8
Jude	Contend for Faith	65–80	Jude	Apostasy	Jude 1:3
Revelation	Triumph of Christ	95	John	Victory	Rev. 21:4

BONUS

Apocalyptic Terms and Theories

I. Core Themes of Biblical Apocalypse

Theme	Description	Key Scriptures
Revelation (Unveiling)	"Apocalypse" (Greek *apokalypsis*) means *unveiling*—a divine disclosure of hidden truths about God's plan for history and the end of the age.	Revelation 1:1; Daniel 2:28
Conflict of Kingdoms	Cosmic struggle between the Kingdom of God and the kingdoms of this world, often symbolized by beasts, empires, or Babylon.	Daniel 7; Revelation 13; Matthew 24
Judgment and Vindication	God judges the wicked and vindicates the righteous; resurrection and eternal destiny follow.	Daniel 12:1–3; Revelation 20
The Day of the Lord	A climactic period of divine intervention bringing both destruction and deliverance.	Joel 2; Zephaniah 1; 2 Peter 3
New Creation	God renews heaven and earth; evil, death, and pain are abolished.	Isaiah 65–66; Revelation 21–22

II. Major Apocalyptic Theories and Interpretations

1. Preterism

- **View:** Most (or all) prophecies in Revelation and Matthew 24 were fulfilled in the first century—especially with the **fall of Jerusalem in AD 70**.
- **Focus:** Symbolic representation of the Roman Empire and early church persecution.
- **Key Figures:** Some Church Fathers (Eusebius), modern theologians like R.C. Sproul (partial preterist).
- **Strengths:** Emphasizes historical context; consistent with "this generation shall not pass" (Matthew 24:34).
- **Criticism:** Downplays the future, global dimension of prophecy.

2. Historicist View

- **View:** Revelation describes **the unfolding of world history** from the early church to the end times.
- **Examples:**
    - The Beast = Papal Rome (Reformation view).
    - The 1,260 days = 1,260 years of papal dominance.
- **Key Figures:** Reformers like Martin Luther, John Calvin, and later Protestant interpreters.
- **Strengths:** Sees prophecy fulfilled across centuries.

- **Criticism:** Can lead to speculation and shifting identifications.

---

3. Futurism

- **View:** Most prophecies in Revelation (especially chs. 4–22) are yet to be fulfilled; concern **a future tribulation, Antichrist, and millennial reign**.
- **Key Ideas:**
    - Seven-year **Tribulation** (Daniel's 70th week).
    - **Antichrist** as a global ruler.
    - **Mark of the Beast** (Revelation 13).
    - **Battle of Armageddon** and Christ's physical return.
- **Key Figures:** John Nelson Darby, Hal Lindsey, Tim LaHaye.
- **Strengths:** Takes future prophecies literally; emphasizes hope in Christ's return.
- **Criticism:** Sometimes overly sensational; relies on speculative timelines.

---

4. Idealist (Symbolic) View

- **View:** Revelation is **not tied to specific historical events** but symbolically portrays the timeless conflict between good and evil.
- **Symbols:** Beast = tyranny, Babylon = worldly corruption, New Jerusalem = ultimate victory of the Church.
- **Key Figures:** Augustine (in part), William Hendriksen.
- **Strengths:** Emphasizes spiritual meaning; relevant in all ages.
- **Criticism:** Lacks concrete predictive value; can seem overly abstract.

---

5. Dispensational Premillennialism

- **View:** History unfolds in **distinct dispensations** or eras. Includes a **pretribulation rapture** of the Church, **7-year tribulation, second coming**, and **literal 1,000-year reign** of Christ on earth.
- **Timeline Example:**
    1. Rapture of believers (1 Thess. 4:16–17)
    2. Tribulation period (Daniel 9:27; Rev. 6–18)
    3. Second Coming of Christ (Revelation 19)
    4. Millennial Kingdom (Revelation 20)
    5. New Heaven and New Earth (Revelation 21–22)
- **Popularized by:** Scofield Bible, *Left Behind* series.
- **Strengths:** Clear chronological framework; literal interpretation.
- **Criticism:** Not held by the early church; highly systematized.

III. Central Apocalyptic Concepts and Symbols

Concept	Meaning / Interpretation	Biblical Source
Beast(s)	Political or religious empires opposed to God.	Daniel 7; Revelation 13
Babylon	Symbol of worldly power, luxury, and corruption.	Revelation 17–18
Antichrist	Ultimate deceiver opposing Christ; possibly individual or system.	1 John 2:18; 2 Thess. 2
Mark of the Beast	Allegiance to Antichrist's system; economic/spiritual submission.	Revelation 13
144,000	Often symbolic of God's covenant people (12 tribes × 12,000).	Revelation 7
New Jerusalem	Eternal dwelling of the redeemed with God.	Revelation 21–22

IV. Apocalyptic Patterns Across Scripture

Book	Apocalyptic Vision	Key Message
Daniel	Four beasts, statue of empires, Son of Man	God's kingdom triumphs over all earthly powers.
Ezekiel	Wheels, temple visions, Gog and Magog	God's glory and restoration of His people.
Isaiah 24–27, 65–66	Judgment and new heavens/new earth	God renews creation after judgment.
Zechariah	Horsemen, lampstand, flying scroll	God's ultimate victory and return to Zion.
Revelation	Seven seals, trumpets, bowls, new creation	Christ conquers evil and reigns forever.

V. Eschatological Timelines (Interpretive Overview)

Event	Pretrib / Futurist View	Amillennial / Idealist View
Rapture	Before Tribulation	Symbolic of believer's union with Christ
Tribulation	Literal 7 years	Represents ongoing persecution
Second Coming	After Tribulation	Single event marking final judgment
Millennium	Literal 1,000 years reign	Symbolic of Church Age
Final Judgment	After Millennium	After symbolic Church Age

COMPARISON OF MAJOR APOCALYPTIC THEORIES

Theory	View of Revelation & Prophecy	Main Events / Focus	Time Focus	Key Scriptures Interpreted
Preterism	Revelation mostly fulfilled in the 1st century (AD 70 destruction of Jerusalem).	Fall of Jerusalem, persecution under Rome, vindication of the Church.	Past	Matthew 24; Luke 21; Revelation 6–18
Historicist	Revelation unfolds through church history (Rome → Middle Ages → Reformation → Modern).	Papacy as Beast, Reformation as divine deliverance, ongoing battle.	Past–Present	Daniel 7; Revelation 13; 17
Futurism	Revelation 4–22 describes future global events before Christ's return.	Rapture, Antichrist, Great Tribulation, Armageddon, Millennium.	Future	Daniel 9:27; Revelation 6–20; Matthew 24
Idealist (Symbolic)	Revelation is a spiritual allegory of the eternal struggle between good and evil.	Ongoing conflict between Church & Satan; ultimate victory of God.	Timeless	Revelation 12; 19–21; Ephesians 6
Dispensational Premillennialism	Literal future timeline divided into dispensations.	Pretribulation Rapture, Tribulation, Second Coming, 1,000-year reign.	Future	1 Thess. 4:16–17; Revelation 19–20

APOCALYPTIC TIMELINE COMPARISON

Event	Preterist View	Historicist View	Futurist / Dispensational View	Idealist / Amillennial View
Church Age	Ends in AD 70	Spans 2,000 years	Ends at Rapture	Symbolic "Millennium" of Christ's rule through the Church
Rapture	Not literal	Not emphasized	Literal catching up of believers before Tribulation	Symbolic of resurrection & union with Christ
Tribulation	Persecution under Rome (AD 64–70)	Church persecution throughout history	7-year literal period under Antichrist	Symbolic of ongoing trials of the Church

Antichrist / Beast	Nero (or Rome)	Papacy or empire	Future world ruler	Symbol of human rebellion against God
Second Coming	Judgment on Jerusalem (AD 70)	Future return at end of history	Visible, bodily return after Tribulation	One final return to judge and renew creation
Millennium (Reign of Christ)	Symbolic—fulfilled in the Church	1,000 years = long period of church dominance	Literal 1,000-year reign after Second Coming	Symbolic of present spiritual reign
Final Judgment	AD 70 or future general judgment	Future final judgment	After Millennium	After Christ's return
New Heaven & New Earth	Spiritual renewal of covenant	Final restoration after history	Eternal state following final judgment	Fulfillment of God's promises—eternal state

SYMBOLS AND THEIR INTERPRETIVE MEANINGS

Symbol	Literal / Futurist Meaning	Symbolic / Idealist Meaning	Historical / Preterist Meaning
Beast	Future Antichrist empire	Political/religious opposition to God	Roman Empire (esp. Nero)
Babylon	End-time world system	Corrupt culture opposed to God	Pagan Rome / Jerusalem
Mark of the Beast (666)	Literal mark or system of allegiance	Symbol of moral/spiritual compromise	Nero's name in Hebrew numerology
New Jerusalem	Future literal city of God	Symbol of God's redeemed people	Fulfillment of the new covenant
Armageddon	Literal final battle in Israel	Symbol of climactic spiritual conflict	Fall of Jerusalem / Rome
Gog & Magog	Nations opposing God after Millennium	Ongoing rebellion of evil forces	Symbolic of ancient enemies of Israel (Ezekiel 38–39)

MAJOR END-TIME EVENTS (Futurist Framework Example)

Here's the **classic dispensational (futurist)** timeline, the one most associated with modern prophecy charts:

1. **The Rapture** — Christ secretly gathers believers (1 Thess. 4:16–17).
2. **Rise of the Antichrist** — Global leader forms a covenant with Israel (Daniel 9:27).
3. **Seven-Year Tribulation** — Divine judgments (seals, trumpets, bowls; Revelation 6–16).
4. **Abomination of Desolation** — Antichrist desecrates the rebuilt temple (Matthew 24:15).
5. **Battle of Armageddon** — Christ returns in glory to defeat evil (Revelation 19).
6. **Millennial Reign** — Christ rules on earth for 1,000 years (Revelation 20).
7. **Final Rebellion and Judgment** — Satan released, final defeat (Revelation 20:7–15).
8. **New Heaven and New Earth** — Eternal state of the redeemed (Revelation 21–22).

CROSS-SCRIPTURE CONNECTIONS (Apocalyptic Network)

Old Testament Prophecy	New Testament Fulfillment / Echo
Daniel 7 (Beasts, Ancient of Days)	Revelation 13, 20 (Beast, final judgment)
Ezekiel 38–39 (Gog and Magog)	Revelation 20:7–10
Joel 2 (Day of the Lord)	Acts 2; Revelation 6–19
Isaiah 65–66 (New Heaven & Earth)	Revelation 21–22
Zechariah 14 (Lord's return on Mount of Olives)	Acts 1:11–12; Revelation 19

Rapture Theories

Rapture theories (or "views of the Rapture") describe different interpretations among Christians about **when and how believers will be taken up to meet Christ** in relation to the **Tribulation** (a future period of suffering and judgment described in prophecy, especially in Daniel and Revelation).

Below is a breakdown of the **main rapture theories**, their biblical basis, and key distinctions:

1. Pre-Tribulation Rapture (Pre-Trib)

Summary:
Believers are "caught up" *before* the 7-year Tribulation begins.

Key Idea:
The Church will not experience God's wrath — the rapture is a rescue before the Tribulation.

Biblical Passages Used:

- 1 Thessalonians 4:16–17 — "the dead in Christ shall rise first… we who are alive… will be caught up."
- 1 Thessalonians 5:9 — "God has not appointed us to wrath."
- Revelation 3:10 — "I will keep you from the hour of trial."

Main Supporters:
Many evangelical and dispensational scholars (e.g., John Walvoord, Tim LaHaye).

Timeline:

1. Rapture → 2. 7-Year Tribulation → 3. Second Coming of Christ → 4. Millennium

---

2. Mid-Tribulation Rapture (Mid-Trib)

Summary:
The Rapture occurs *in the middle* of the 7-year Tribulation — after the first 3½ years but before the "Great Tribulation."

Key Idea:
The Church will experience some persecution, but will be taken before the outpouring of God's wrath in the final half.

Biblical Passages Used:

- Daniel 9:27 — divides the Tribulation into two halves.
- Revelation 11:11–12 — the two witnesses are caught up mid-Trib.
- 1 Corinthians 15:52 — "at the last trumpet" (interpreted as mid-point trumpet).

Timeline:

1. 3½ years (first half of Tribulation) → **Rapture** → 3½ years (Great Tribulation) → Second Coming

3. Post-Tribulation Rapture (Post-Trib)

Summary:
The Rapture and the Second Coming are the *same event* — the Church goes through the entire Tribulation and is caught up to meet Christ as He descends to earth.

Key Idea:
Believers are protected *through* the Tribulation, not taken out of it.

Biblical Passages Used:

- Matthew 24:29–31 — "Immediately after the tribulation… he will send his angels to gather his elect."
- John 16:33 — "In this world you will have tribulation."
- Revelation 20:4–6 — saints who endured tribulation reign with Christ.

Timeline:

1. 7-Year Tribulation → **Rapture/Second Coming (same event)** → Millennium

---

4. Pre-Wrath Rapture

Summary:
The Rapture happens *after* most of the Tribulation but *before* God's direct wrath is poured out (around the sixth seal of Revelation).

Key Idea:
The Church experiences persecution from Satan and the Antichrist but not the divine wrath of God.

Biblical Passages Used:

- Matthew 24:21–31 — distress followed by gathering of the elect.
- Revelation 6–8 — believers are raptured before the "Day of the Lord."
- 1 Thessalonians 5:9 — believers spared from God's wrath.

Timeline:

1. Early Tribulation (Satan's wrath) → **Rapture (before God's wrath)** → Day of the Lord judgments → Second Coming

5. Partial Rapture Theory

Summary:
Only *faithful* or *watchful* Christians are raptured before the Tribulation; others are left to endure it and may be taken later.

Key Idea:
The Rapture is a reward for readiness and spiritual preparedness.

Biblical Passages Used:

- Matthew 25:1–13 — the wise and foolish virgins.
- Luke 21:36 — "pray that you may be counted worthy to escape."
- Revelation 3:10 — conditional promise of deliverance.

Timeline:
Multiple raptures may occur based on believers' readiness.

---

6. Pan-Tribulation View (Humorous/Practical View)

Summary:
"It'll all pan out in the end."
This view expresses humility — that the exact timing is less important than being spiritually ready whenever Christ returns.

Comparison Table

View	When Rapture Occurs	Believers Experience Tribulation?	Key Verse(s)
Pre-Trib	Before Tribulation	No	1 Thess. 4:16–17; Rev. 3:10
Mid-Trib	Midpoint (3½ years)	Partially	Dan. 9:27; Rev. 11:11–12
Pre-Wrath	Before God's Wrath (late Trib.)	Yes (early part)	Matt. 24:21–31; 1 Thess. 5:9
Post-Trib	After Tribulation	Yes	Matt. 24:29–31; Rev. 20:4–6
Partial	Varies (based on faithfulness)	Some	Matt. 25:1–13; Luke 21:36

Rapture Theories and the Book of Revelation

1. Pre-Tribulation View

Core Idea:
The Church is taken up *before* the Tribulation (Revelation chapters 6–19), which primarily concerns Israel and unbelievers.

Revelation Connections:

Passage	Interpretation
Revelation 3:10 – "I will keep you from the hour of trial."	The "hour of trial" = 7-year Tribulation. Promise of removal before it begins.
Revelation 4:1 – "Come up here."	John's ascent to heaven is seen as a *symbolic picture* of the Rapture (the Church no longer mentioned after ch. 3).
Revelation 6–19	Seen as God's wrath poured out on earth after the Church's removal.
Revelation 19:11–16	Christ returns *with* the saints — indicating they were already with Him.

Summary Timeline:
Church Age → Rapture (Rev 4:1) → Tribulation (Rev 6–19) → Second Coming (Rev 19)

---

2. Mid-Tribulation View

Core Idea:
The Rapture occurs *midway through* the Tribulation — around the **seventh trumpet**.

Revelation Connections:

Passage	Interpretation
Revelation 11:11–12 – The two witnesses are resurrected and caught up to heaven.	This event mirrors the rapture — symbolizing believers' ascension at the midpoint.
Revelation 11:15 – "The seventh trumpet sounded…"	Identified with "the last trumpet" in 1 Corinthians 15:52.
Revelation 12	Depicts spiritual warfare and Israel's flight — events occurring mid-Tribulation.

Summary Timeline:
First 3½ years → **Rapture (7th Trumpet)** → Great Tribulation → Second Coming

3. Pre-Wrath View

Core Idea:
The Rapture happens *late in the Tribulation*, but *before* God's direct wrath (the "Day of the Lord") begins — roughly between the **sixth and seventh seals**.

Revelation Connections:

Passage	Interpretation
Revelation 6:12–17 – Sixth seal: cosmic signs and the declaration, "The great day of His wrath has come."	Believers raptured *before* this wrath is poured out.
Revelation 7:9–14 – "A great multitude… came out of the great tribulation."	Represents raptured saints now in heaven.
Revelation 8–16 – Trumpet and bowl judgments = outpouring of divine wrath following the Rapture.	

Summary Timeline:
Tribulation (man's/Antichrist's wrath) → **Rapture (Rev 6–7)** → God's Wrath (Rev 8–16) → Second Coming

4. Post-Tribulation View

Core Idea:
The Rapture and the Second Coming are *the same event* — occurring *after* the Tribulation when Christ returns to reign.

Revelation Connections:

Passage	Interpretation
Revelation 6–18	Church endures persecution through the Tribulation.
Revelation 19:11–16 – Christ returns on a white horse.	This is both the Second Coming *and* the Rapture — believers rise to meet Him and immediately return with Him.
Revelation 20:4–6 – Saints who suffered reign with Christ.	Evidence that believers experienced the Tribulation.

Summary Timeline:
Tribulation (Rev 6–18) → **Rapture/Second Coming (Rev 19)** → Millennium (Rev 20)

5. Partial Rapture View

Core Idea:
Only faithful believers are raptured early; others endure part or all of the Tribulation and are taken later.

Revelation Connections:

Passage	Interpretation
Revelation 3:10 – "I will keep you from the hour of trial."	Applied conditionally to "overcomers."
Revelation 7; 14:1–5	Multiple groups of redeemed believers appear at different times, suggesting staggered raptures.
Revelation 19:7–9	The Bride (faithful Church) is in heaven before the return, implying others may come later.

6. The "Pan-Trib" (It'll All Pan Out) View

Core Idea:
Because Revelation is filled with symbolism, some believers focus less on *timing* and more on *readiness*.
Christ's call in Revelation 16:15 sums it up:

"Behold, I come as a thief. Blessed is he who watches, and keeps his garments."

Summary Table — Revelation-Based Rapture Theories

Theory	Key Revelation Chapters	Timing of Rapture	View of the Church's Role
Pre-Trib	Rev 3–4	Before Tribulation	Church absent from Tribulation
Mid-Trib	Rev 11	Middle (7th Trumpet)	Church experiences first half
Pre-Wrath	Rev 6–7	Before God's Wrath	Church endures Antichrist's persecution
Post-Trib	Rev 19	After Tribulation	Church endures full Tribulation
Partial	Various (Rev 3, 7, 14)	Multiple points	Faithful taken early; others later

The Abomination That Causes Desolation

Original Term (Hebrew):
שִׁקּוּץ שֹׁמֵם (*shiqqûts shômêm*)
Literally: "A detestable or idolatrous thing that brings ruin or devastation."

The phrase combines:

- **Abomination (shiqqûts):** something idolatrous or sacrilegious, offensive to God.
- **Desolation (shômêm):** devastation, ruin, or emptiness.

So together it means:

"A defiling act or object that brings spiritual and physical devastation to the holy place."

First Appearance — Daniel's Prophecy

The phrase originates in the **Book of Daniel**, which lays the foundation for all later end-time prophecy.

Verse	Reference	Summary
Daniel 9:27	"He shall confirm a covenant with many for one week… but in the middle of the week he shall bring an end to sacrifice and offering; and on the wing of abominations shall be one who makes desolate."	A ruler breaks a 7-year covenant and desecrates the temple.
Daniel 11:31	"Forces from him shall appear and profane the temple… they shall set up the abomination that makes desolate."	Refers to a historical act of sacrilege (see below).
Daniel 12:11	"From the time that the regular burnt offering is taken away and the abomination that makes desolate is set up…"	Tied to end-time events and specific days (1,290).

3. Historical Fulfillment — Antiochus IV Epiphanes (168 BC)

Many scholars identify a **partial fulfillment** in the actions of **Antiochus IV Epiphanes**, a Greek ruler during the intertestamental period.

- He invaded Jerusalem (168 BC).
- **Desecrated the Jewish Temple** by erecting an altar to **Zeus** and sacrificing a **pig** on the altar of burnt offering.

- Outlawed Jewish worship and forced idol sacrifices.

This was the **historical "abomination"** Daniel foresaw — but **Jesus later spoke of it as future**, showing it was a **foreshadowing** of a greater event still to come.

---

4. Jesus' Prophecy — Matthew 24:15

"So when you see standing in the holy place 'the abomination that causes desolation,' spoken of through the prophet Daniel — let the reader understand…"
— *Matthew 24:15 (see also Mark 13:14)*

Here, Jesus:

- **Confirms Daniel's prophecy** as legitimate and not fully fulfilled.
- Places its ultimate fulfillment **in the future**, connected to **the Great Tribulation**.
- Warns believers in Judea to flee when it occurs — indicating it marks a turning point in end-time events.

---

5. Future Fulfillment — The Antichrist

In **end-time prophecy**, particularly **Revelation 13** and **2 Thessalonians 2:3–4**, the **"abomination of desolation"** is connected with the **Antichrist**.

How it unfolds (according to prophetic interpretation):

Event	Description	Key Scriptures
1. Covenant confirmed	The Antichrist makes or strengthens a 7-year peace covenant with Israel.	Daniel 9:27a
2. Midpoint betrayal	After 3½ years, he breaks the covenant and enters the rebuilt Temple.	Daniel 9:27b; Matt. 24:15
3. Desecration of the Temple	He sets up an image of himself, demands worship, and halts sacrifices.	2 Thess. 2:4; Rev. 13:14–15
4. Great Tribulation begins	This event marks the start of the final 3½ years — the "Great Tribulation."	Matt. 24:21; Rev. 13:5–7

This act — the Antichrist declaring himself as God in the Temple — is the future "abomination that causes desolation."

6. Relation to Rapture Theories

Rapture Theory	How It Relates to the "Abomination of Desolation"
Pre-Tribulation	Believers are raptured **before** the Antichrist's revelation and the abomination.
Mid-Tribulation	The **abomination marks the midpoint** — the moment of the Rapture.
Pre-Wrath	The abomination begins the **Great Tribulation**, and the Rapture happens **sometime after**, before God's wrath.
Post-Tribulation	Believers endure through the abomination and are raptured **after** the Tribulation.

7. Theological Significance

The abomination that causes desolation represents:

- **Ultimate rebellion against God** — humanity worshiping itself in the place of God.
- **Desecration of what is holy** — turning worship into idolatry.
- **Trigger of divine judgment** — it signals the beginning of the most intense period of tribulation.

8. Summary Timeline (Prophetic)

Time	Event
1. Start of 7-Year Tribulation	Covenant with Israel (Dan. 9:27a)
2. Midpoint (3½ years)	**Abomination of Desolation** — Antichrist in Temple (Matt. 24:15)
3. Final 3½ years	Great Tribulation (Matt. 24:21)
4. End of Tribulation	Second Coming of Christ (Matt. 24:29–30; Rev. 19:11–16)

PRE-TEST ANSWERS

1. Name two Patriarchs? There are 4 patriarchs: Abraham, Isaac, Jacob and Joseph

2. How many books are in the Old Testament? 39
3. Psalms is divided into how many sections? 5
4. Who wrote the largest number of books in the Old Testament? Moses wrote the first 5 books of the old testament.
5. Who was the first prophet in the Old Testament? Samuel
6. Name one of God's covenantal names? Jehovah Jirah, Rapha, Nissi, Tsidkenu, Shalom etc....
7. Who was the 1st King of Israel? King Saul
8. Write one scripture in the book of psalms?

9. What is the longest book in the Old Testament? Psalms
10. Who was the richest King in the Old Testament? King Solomon
11. Who is known as "a man after God's own heart?" King David
12. What is the difference between the major and the minor prophets?
The length of the book and the volume of prophecy

13. Which book of the bible focuses on the Holy Spirit? Acts
14. What is the purpose of the gospels?
To share the good news and speak of the works of Jesus

15. How many books are in the New Testament? 27
16. What is an Epistle? A letter written by the apostles

17. Name two epistles?

18. How many gospels are there? 4
19. Who wrote the largest number of books in the New Testament? Apostle Paul
20. What is an apostle? A sent one

21. Name 4 key figures in the New Testament? Jesus, Holy Spirit, Matthew, Mark, Luke etc.

Bibliography

1. M. G. Easton: Easton's Bible Dictionary - Christian Classics Ethereal Library
   https://ccel.org/ccel/easton/ebd2/ebd2.html?term=Prophet
2. John Walton: Chronological and Background Charts of the Old Testament
3. Pamela Vinnett: Prophetic Protocol A Practical Handbook on the Prophets Mantle
4. Hendrickson Publishers Marketing LLC: The Complete Jewish Study Bible
5. Tamiya D. Lewis: Prayer 101 Training Manual
6. https://chatgpt.com/
7. https://gemini.google.com/

www.ingramcontent.com/pod-product-compliance
Lightning Source LLC
Chambersburg PA
CBHW081159020426
42333CB00020B/2558